Twin Flames and How They Change Your World

Maura Lawler

BALBOA.PRESS
A DIVISION OF HAY HOUSE

Balboa Press books may be ordered through booksellers or by contacting:

Balboa Press
A Division of Hay House
1663 Liberty Drive
Bloomington, IN 47403
www.balboapress.com
844-682-1282

Print information available on the last page.

ISBN: 979-8-7652-5555-1 (sc)
ISBN: 979-8-7652-5554-4 (e)

Balboa Press rev. date: 09/23/2024

Acknowledgments

First and foremost, I would like to thank Ellen Bitterman, my editor, who worked her magic in her way over the past five years (since 2018), helping me to create and recreate the chapters of this book. Thank you for your professional guidance, understanding and trust throughout the many stages of bringing this book into form.

I am grateful for the opportunity to have met Bob Cirame and for the life lessons that prompted me to write this book.

I am ever grateful to my son Youssef, now embarking on his teen years, who has always been a guiding light for me, a beacon and beautiful spirit that unfolds and grows in such extraordinary ways more and more every year. You are wiser than your years would suggest.

And to Abdul Karradi, thanks for the life lessons I have learned throughout the years without which I would not be who I am.

Words of appreciation fall short in expressing my gratitude to Charles Connor, always Charley to me, my twin flame and my muse whom I met eight years ago. Our twin flame journey ignited the very writing of this book, and it is in large part a story of my twin flame journey with Charley whose presence in my life has been beyond worldly measure.

So many thanks to all of you in the twin flame community and the many people I have met along the twin flame journey for their unconditional love and support. And to the magic of the awakening process that is found within the twin flame community and the sharing of experiences of deep meaning and connection that unite us all in awakening and love.

Special words of thanks go out to my family and friends. To my dad and mom for the wisdom and life lessons they imparted. So much gratitude to Paul Denniston, my grief yoga teacher for reminding me to sit with discomfort and let things flow; to my writing teacher Andrea Cagan for encouraging me to continue writing; and to David Kessler, my grief education teacher, for always reminding me that in life we must *go through* our challenges and *not around* them!

To my therapist, thank you for helping me weave through the intricate parts of this journey.

I am also grateful to those who contributed their unique talents to this book—my friend Chad LaMarsh for letting me use some of his music and cover designer David Rival for his artistic talent and creative contribution.

And last but certainly not least . . . Thank you to the universe and my angels above for always encouraging me to put one foot in front of the other—quitting was never an option! It was and always will be a journey coming home to self and to those you love.

Charlie Kanelos – Thank you to helping me to find my voice through music and the choir not to dim my light.

Michael Auclair – Thank you for your Wisdom, Friendship and laughter and for reminding me not to take life too seriously. Thank you for always reminding me to find humor.

Lisa Ponte - Thank you for continued support and for encouraging me to complete this book. Very grateful to have met you.

About the cover of the book

Even though the candle on the front cover is a religious symbol. The candle I felt reminded me of the twin flame connection as the flames coming together as one. The alpha omega on the candle reminds me of the ying yang symbol of the spiritual in the twin flame connection. This is why I chose this as I felt it reminded me of Christ Consciousness no matter what religion you are as the twin flame connection is a spiritual connection that helps to balance the alpha omega/ying yang in all of us.

About the Book/Summary

Twin Flames and How They Change Your World by Maura Lawler is about the coming home to oneself as you unravel a remembrance of who you are. It is also about the awakening experience once you are awakened by your Twin Flame and the roller coaster of emotions that can feel overwhelming at times as you learn to balance the irrational and logic parts of your mind in order for the heart to catch up as love always resides in the heart. The Twin Flame Connection is a soul heart awakening and one that can never be lost on all dimensions, despite what lessons we are meant to learn in the physical, we are always connected as one through the heart and soul with our Twin Flame.

Contents

CHAPTER 1

Meeting Your Twin Flame

It all started back in August of 2015. The day when you get the postcard in the mail and the postcard says who your child's teacher is. Well, I kept looking at the postcard with so much recognition. I then finally say I know this guy from somewhere. I then say to my son, "Well, you will be in awesome hands."

Rewind back to three years earlier when my son was one year old. I was looking to buy a house and had looked in Newton, Massachusetts, at two places which would have been a block away from where my twin currently lives. Ultimately, I bought a house in Needham, Massachusetts, where my twin flame taught. You can say that I always felt him around, but I guess, as they say you have to learn life lessons along the way. My twin flame and I have always worked or lived close, about ten to fifteen minutes away from each other, for the last thirty years. We have always lived worlds apart but yet so close.

A few years after I had moved to Needham, a majority of the time I would always be pulled to go grocery shopping in Newton near where my twin flame lives. Some days I would wonder why I would be pulled to go grocery shopping in the town he lived in although I did not know he lived there at the time. Also, in Needham we have three grocery stores, so I always felt pulled to meet him, but if you have blocks that need to be cleared, then God and the universe will not let you meet in the physical until you are ready to heal.

Now fast forward back to September of 2015 when I went on this family vacation with my family and I felt I was not meant to go on this vacation as my passport had expired and I had to get an emergency passport to fly the next day. Also, my suitcase gave way last minute and everything fell out of it. When I finally got to my destination, I had an intense dream of my twin flame and I yelled and shouted out that I wanted to go home and be with him. We finally got home from our vacation in October 2015, and I could feel my life change from then on. Then, came December of 2015 when my twin had a cold and cough. I also had a cold and cough that lingered, and I tried every medication but none worked. This indicated to me how my twin and I were connected as we were both sick in December of 2015, the year we met in the physical, and again in December 2016. This is when I had heard that when you are strongly connected to your twin energetically, you both can experience having the flu simultaneously.

Then came February of 2016, when my twin and I were in the meeting room for my son's IEP meeting and that is when we looked into each other's eyes and the room felt so silenced. It felt as though we were the only ones in the meeting room. From February 2016, I began lying awake at night knowing I was married, having feelings for this man. I kept fighting my feelings in every way. Everything I thought logical seemed illogical. Then came spring of 2016 when I nominated my twin for an award. You would have thought when I got asked to write something about his nomination, I could have written a book back then.

Then came May of 2016 when I walked out of the school where my twin taught, vibrating from head to toe, hoping no one was passing judgment on me. From this day on, I felt the town where I lived was judging me, but I know that was just my ego I was clinging to. Then came the summer of 2016, when I felt I was suffering something psychological as my twin and I did not have much communication, and I did not know what I was experiencing at the time. We, as humans, tend to think when something changes in our life that immediately we are suffering something psychological. There were days that I felt I needed to check myself into a hospital. I was determined to work through these emotions one way or another. I prayed for a way to talk to someone. That is when I came upon California Psychics, Abby, Delano, Ladonna, Edie, and Tenley, who helped me significantly.

I spoke with California Psychics over the phone. Then, in July I was connected to Delano, who was able to describe my twin in detail. I am forever grateful to Delano, who helped talk me off a ledge. I still prayed for a place I could go to and get the support necessary. Then, an advertisement to Uplifting Connections in Bridgewater, MA came on my Facebook feed. I finally decided to go there in October of 2016; here I met Jon and Kellie the owners. Then, I met Debbie McBride and Lisa Ashton, who I first began seeing for reiki treatment, a healing modality that helps with energy work. Then, I met Lisa Brazil-Pomar, with whom I continued my reiki sessions. In January of 2017, she started a journaling class. We had and still have so many journal prompts about anger, forgiveness, life, sadness, happiness, and letting go. This really has helped me in grounding my thoughts.

Then in the spring of 2017, I was lying awake at night and saw a profound vision of a book called *Twin Flames and How They Change Your World*. I started to question this, as the more I saw the vision, the more I meditated on it and then I knew—I had to write this book to help other twin flames on this journey. The twin flame experience is an awesome, amazing gift from God. There are so many blessings along the way on this journey, and you definitely have to be a tough soul to take it on. The twin flame journey is a journey of loving ourselves completely and not needing a partner or anything outside of ourselves to complete us. The journey is about how we are able to thrive in this society on our own and not be codependent with someone or something. We as a society often portray that we need to be codependent with someone or something to complete us and that we do not know how to manage on our own. I will give you an example as my twin was a preschool teacher; he taught the children how to share and/or wait for the particular toy or book they want and not to need to be in control and be dependent on the object that they desire.

One other thing I mentioned about the pull to your twin flame is that long before I met my twin in the physical, I was pulled to go to church in Needham, MA. Not realizing years later after meeting my twin that he played the organ at Saint Bartholomew Church at mass. One piece of advice I want to give is that when your soul is being pushed to meet your twin flame or to try something new, we all never know why; as I said before, we get pulled to do or meet the people we are supposed to meet. Meeting your twin flame reminds you of the feelings and bond you have between one another. Twin flames also represent the acceptance of self. Loving all parts of yourself and your twin without words or pretenses. Throughout the twin flame journey, it is always about bringing you back to self-love and knowing you are capable of anything. Also, to love yourself, God, and your twin flame unconditionally through all levels of growth and to remind us that we do not need people's approval to be who we are and what we came here on this Earth to accomplish.

Do you believe you have met your twin flame? Remember back to Romeo and Juliet and their forbidden love for one another. They knew in their souls they were meant for each other despite obstacles that got in the way. Some people wonder if they should go looking for their twin flame. Your twin will show up in unexpected places. I know this because my twin flame was my son's preschool teacher. Twin flames are one soul in two bodies. Twin flames incarnate on this Earth from the moment they are born. Twin flames are a sacred marriage on a spiritual level. Twin flames share the same soul essence and energetic blueprint. The twin flame experience can be extremely powerful, heart-wrenching and challenging. It is meant for you and your twin to be able to grow and transform on many levels. When you meet your twin flame, you feel a sense of belonging and a connection like no other. Once you meet your twin flame, as I have, that is when the healing begins as you and your twin flame are connected on an energetic level. You can have the physical relationship, but you need to heal a lot of wounds that you have carried with you from lifetime to lifetime and to let go of what no longer serves you. Throughout life, as I mentioned previously, you can always feel your twin flame around. I have felt my twin around me for the last thirty years. If there are blocks that need to be healed, God and the universe will not let you meet your twin flame until you are both ready to heal. The twin flame is a blessing. You and your twin help one another become the best versions of yourselves. I am thankful to God each day that I have met my twin flame.

Another memory I have long before I met my twin flame back in the 1990s is when my cousin was married in Washington, D.C. When I was at my cousin's wedding, I felt this huge pull to explore the Washington, D.C./Maryland area. I later found out that my twin flame had grown up in this area. As I mentioned, all throughout life, you will always have a pull to someone or something and when you meet your twin flame in the physical, you will eventually understand with more clarity why you had the pull. A twin flame relationship is not about the physical romance at first, but rather it is about the higher purpose that twin flames came here to accomplish. This does not mean you won't have a great relationship in the physical eventually, but that you both must fulfill a higher calling. Meeting your twin flame is one of the most powerful experiences you will have in your life. Your twin flame is someone with whom you share complete trust and feel a sense of inner strength and expansion. Your world literally changes in every way.

When I met my twin flame for the first time, it was soul recognition. I felt butterflies in my stomach as if I were a teenager falling in love all over again. Deep down inside I felt as if I had known my twin flame for an eternity. One thing I also remember as I am back into writing my book is that I woke up to a song literally playing in my head and thought that I had left the song playing on my radio, but then I realized it was a dream of my friend Chad LaMarsh's song called "Reason to Breathe." I feel it was a reminder that God gave us a reason to be here to accomplish our life purpose and not to shy away from our gifts and talents and that God and our twin flames are our biggest mirrors and they remind us as well. This song was really significant to me when I woke up to my friend's song in my head as people at any point can totally pull you from your path. You and only you are in control of your destiny and getting back on track and accomplishing your dreams and desires. When meeting your twin flame, you feel as though the lights have come on and you start to see life with more clarity. As you meet your twin flame, you start to let go of the past, opening your heart and becoming vulnerable. You also find the courage to be yourself.

In July of 2017 when I finally talked to my twin flame about our connection, I experienced tremendous vulnerability. It was scary, but it was a risk I had to take. I kept talking myself out of talking with my twin flame about our connection. I realized that you need to trust yourself and your true feelings for your twin. Your feelings for your twin flame do not magically disappear. Once you are able to find the courage and honor to work on your soul's truth with God, you, and your twin flame, it will help you tremendously. I encourage you to talk openly to your twin flame. Twin flames find each other as they recognize one another on a deep soul-to-soul level. Upon meeting your twin flame there is an instant connection and familiarity as the eyes are the windows to the soul. You can recognize your twin flame when you look into his/her eyes as I did or encounter something that is his/hers, such as the postcard my twin sent out to let the students know who their preschool teacher would be. When meeting your twin, it can feel all bliss. Because of the unique connection there are times that it can feel intense as you start to trigger one another. That is when the healing begins on all core levels. A twin flame is a person who you are destined to feel connected to on a physical, emotional, mental, and spiritual level. When first meeting your twin flame you have a feeling of having met before, as if you knew your twin in a past life.

This definitely happened to me when I met my twin flame, Charles Connor, as well as when I met my twin flame's sister Pat at his retirement party. I had the same feeling of connection with her as well. The twin flame relationship is also like finding inner wholeness. The twin flame journey is about uniting all aspects of yourself, becoming whole within, and accepting both your feminine and masculine side.

Meeting your twin flame feels like an earthquake as it shakes everything up inside of you. The spiritual connection with your twin is magnetic. At times, when you are with your twin flame, you become speechless or are in awe of one another. Another important thing to remember is that the twin flame journey raises both of your awareness and brings you back to Christ Consciousness. Throughout the twin flame journey, you will experience a magnetic pull towards one another, as I explained earlier in this chapter, as I could always feel my twin around and had the pull towards him. As I mentioned previously, if you and your twin have energetic blocks that need to be healed, then God will wait for you to meet to let the healing begin. One thing to keep in mind is that as much as we twins want the physical relationship, we have to remember that the twin flame experience is meant to awaken your senses, talents, and levels of consciousness.

If you encounter a twin flame in this lifetime, as I have, just keep in mind that it can feel as if you are suffering something psychological or a mid-life crisis. Just know you are not and that the right kind of energy work will help you get through this journey one day, one moment, and one second at a time. Eventually, as you go along the twin flame journey, your path to enlightenment will become clearer as you take on this journey one step at a time. Whether or not you reunite in the physical with one another, you are always uniquely connected to one another. You help each other along the way by giving one another strength, guidance, and inspiration, awakening more talents and abilities in one another. You will also learn along the way the meaning of value and challenges to oneness. Once you have fully accepted loving yourself and your twin unconditionally, then you are making more room for expansion and growth. A twin flame experience also helps you to become more compassionate and to continually love all parts of yourself. The journey is always about God, you, and your twin flame and how to bring more love to the world and be able to become a brand-new version of yourself for you, God, and your twin. A twin flame relationship is the most powerful one you will encounter in this lifetime. Your twin flame does not try and change you. You accept one another for who you are. Just like the song by Billy Joel, "Just the Way You Are." I feel this is a great reference as it shows that twins love one another unconditionally, yet they are here or we are here to help each other grow and aspire. A twin flame is your best friend, lover, teacher, and muse all in one. You will find that you will find inner expansion as you grow on the twin flame journey.

CHAPTER 2

Mirror Work

Mirror work is looking at oneself in the mirror and repeating positive affirmations. I am writing about mirror work, as our twin flames and the rest of the world are our mirrors. Most importantly, twin flames share the same soul essence and energy, so that is why mirror work is an important component to healing on the twin flame journey. We, as twins, trigger lots of core wounds in one another. For example, a twin flame could trigger in you a childhood dream you wanted to fulfill, but people told you otherwise, that you were not capable of going to a certain college or working in a certain job. Basically, our twin flame helps us let go of all limiting beliefs that are with us from childhood. Triggers can range from anger, jealousy, and feelings of being inadequate to many childhood wounds. Some people do not realize, when they meet their twin flame, it is a blessing from God because this is when the healing can occur on many levels, the healing of the wounds we have been carrying over from lifetime to lifetime.

The more you can work on healing and mirror work on the twin flame journey the better, as all twin flames came here to bring love, joy, and wisdom to the Earth and to help us let go of negative people, events, or situations that have held us down lifetime after lifetime. I know once you fully accept and receive the blessings from God through the mirror work and let go of a lot of limiting beliefs, you can have the life you want. One thing about doing mirror work is to not hold on to resistance. We, as humans, are taught at a young age that it is not safe to let go, and, therefore, we try to have a tight grip and control over things and people.

This can lead to unhealthy behavior patterns. We, as twin flames, are learning from one another, through the mirror exercise, how to love ourselves completely and become whole within ourselves. Through the mirror work, we are learning to resolve core wounds on every level. We learn that we can be in loving relationships with ourselves and with our twins without being codependent on one another; thus, we can become the best version of ourselves. Through the mirror work, it is important to practice self-care along the way, as you are purging and upheaving a lot of old limiting beliefs.

It is important to practice self-care daily. Remember to work through daily affirmations on a continual basis. During the mirror work, you will learn to peel back layers and layers of old programming. My advice to you is to be patient with yourself and with your twin flame through this process of peeling back layers of old programming. An example of twin flame mirror work is when your twin flame is running from him/herself, and then, in turn, you are running from yourself. Mirror work allows you to be able to dig deep on every core level, to be able to work through why you are running from yourself. Twin flames need to be able to clear negativity on a deeper level. The mirror work is an integral part of this process.

Twin flames mirror one another finding wholeness through the mirror of the soul. When twin flames meet, your twin is the brightest mirror reflecting back to you everything from your deepest core wounds. Meeting your twin flame is a gift, as you are given a chance through God to heal all deep wounds. Sometimes it may seem that your twin does not appreciate you. As twins, we do appreciate one another, but we are also reflecting what needs to be worked on in order to achieve forward movement or growth. Twins show each other how strong and capable you both are. Your twin flame will mirror back to you when you are being codependent. Codependency does not exist in a twin flame relationship. You are not here to save your twin, and he/she is not here to save you, but instead to share the experience of a blissful, joyous, loving relationship. Through the mirror work, we work on self-acceptance through daily affirmations. Loving ourselves fully enough not to have to seek anything outside of ourselves to make us happy. Happiness comes from within.

Mirror work also shows you your shadow side where you have been subservient and how to let go of people who have control over you. It is not okay for a person to control another individual or situations just because a person thinks he/she knows better. I know that often our society portrays the idea that we must control someone or something to get what we want. That is an unhealthy pattern. Regardless of anyone's situation, God gave us all a voice to speak out for what we want for ourselves in order to create a life we desire, rather than a life which someone wants or thinks is best for us. In order to help you heal on a deeper core level, your twin flame will reflect back onto you in harsh, but helpful, ways your unhealthy behaviors when you let other people dictate your wants and needs. The mirror work will help you and your twin understand and explore why you have a lot of anger. Many twins feel anger toward the twin when, in actuality, your twin is pointing out where you are not showing up for yourself which then, in turn, can cause you to be angry with yourself. Your twin will keep reflecting back the instances when you are not showing up for yourself by continuing to let people dictate or run your life until you are ready to heal the core wound.

My twin has shown me a lot of mirror work, especially when I have not shown up for myself and have been subservient or had feelings of jealousy in my life. In the end, there is no room for either of these patterns in any type of relationship and especially in a twin flame relationship dynamic. My twin flame has also reflected back to me some of my negative behavior patterns, when I have not stood up for myself, for what I believe, and for what I want to accomplish in this lifetime. Twin flames will reflect this in harsh ways until we are ready to take back control of our own lives. As I mentioned in Chapter 1, you can ultimately have a relationship with your twin but the old belief systems you have held on to must be cleared away. As you start to work on energy clearing, you must first have a full understanding about how to clear every block on all core levels. Just remember, as I said earlier in this chapter, to give yourself self-love as you do the work of clearing out many old limiting beliefs. Just remember who you are and who the person is who you came here to be. Be there for yourself and keep loving yourself consistently through all the affirmations.

We, as human beings, tend not to want to sit with our feelings. At some point or another we are taught to sweep our feelings and emotions under the rug, so when you see your twin reflect back to you, you have not healed. Remember: it is in your power to heal all aspects of your life. Instead of facing our feelings head on, we tend to run from feelings, and we have a hard time just to sit with them. Once you have completely healed through the mirror work, then you can come into union with God and reunion with your twin flame. As I said in Chapter 1, when meeting your twin flame, it feels all bliss at first. Then, once God and the universe decide when healing begins, it is not all a bed of roses as you and your twin are made for each other to help heal and continually work on blocks that have kept you stuck and impeded you from moving forward in your life purpose from one lifetime to the next. Having the opportunity to know and love your twin flame is also meant to help you to stand in the power of you and not let negative people dull your shine. Again, when you meet your twin flame, you meet when you are in darkness and once you have realized who your twin is to you, the lights start to come on and you start to see life with more clarity. Your shine starts to become brighter as you progress on healing through mirror work and the other healing modalities that you have chosen.

After my twin flame and I had separated in the summer of 2017, I became reiki 1 certified. This modality has helped me to achieve balance. I suggest to you to find a modality that can help you attain balance in your life. Always remember this journey is about God, you, and your twin and remember your power center when people try and pull you from the path. Through the mirror work, you find your voice and how to communicate more effectively with yourself, God, and your twin. Also, through the mirror exercises, God will bring you tests to test your faith and trust, to show how you can be a strong human being without having to control or be controlled by anyone. God gave us power to be who we came here to be and not to have anyone dictate our life. The mirror work is there for you and your twin flame to work through shortcomings because on a spiritual plane, you are your twin and your twin is you. My twin flame and I both are easily able to trigger one another when we are not living up to our truest potential and not honoring ourselves. When meeting your twin flame, you both will mirror a lot of similar experiences that have led you down the same path. When working through the mirror work and either you or your twin flame are running from the connection because of the intensity, honor where you and your twin are at with healing as it helps you both grow spiritually. You do not need to take it personally as we all get caught in our egos. If you are an empath, as I am, some of us take the process of healing more personally than others. All in all, the moral is to honor where you and your twin are at on your healing journey as that is when patience comes in. As I mentioned, our twins are our greatest mirrors, so if we do not have patience for where we both are on this journey, then our twins will mirror us by being impatient and we will, in turn, mirror them with impatience as well.

Furthermore, as you are doing the mirror work, feelings of unworthiness, low self-esteem, depression, and anxiety may arise. It is helpful to know how to work through the mirror work and to follow through with affirmations such as *I am loved, I am smart, I am creative.* Practicing the mirror work can and will work if you are consistent with it. Knowing God is part of the journey, and when you feel your faith and trust have been tested many times on this journey, you and your twin will constantly mirror these feelings in one another until you completely and fully surrender to the journey. Also, part of the journey includes plenty of upheaval and purging.

From my experience when you feel you are abandoned by your twin or by God, they or we ourselves are showing each other how we can be gentle with ourselves, our twin, and God. God reminded me of this in a song that my twin played on the organ one day at mass called "Gentle Woman." This song reminds me of how gentle we have to be to ourselves, our twins, God, and the outside world of people who are not so spiritually evolved. We are reminded that we came here to serve God and one another and the mirror exercise is the most important component to this journey. We are also reminded that if we are going to heal the world, we need to heal within. All too often we forget that this journey is about Christ Consciousness and that God is our greatest protector. He wants what we want as long as we are patient and trust God along this journey. All too often throughout life, we were told by people that if we did not conform to their ways, we felt threatened and in fear. In reality, deep down we know that God is the one who has the control over all of us. Just as the song, "Unwritten," by Natasha Bedingfield mentions that we are the ones who create our reality and that we have the power to make choices for ourselves and live the life we want. The only one that can do the inner work is you through God, and the more you do your inner work and create the reality that you want for yourself, the more doors will open for you and your twin.

Through the mirror work we are learning how to let go of beliefs that no longer serve us. We were told that we were one way and that we were only able to achieve a certain status when, in actuality, we are limitless and can achieve and move forward in any direction we choose. In the beginning when you meet your twin flame, you and your twin flame mirror the love vibration. When going through the mirror work, as I said, you want to be gentle and compassionate with yourself first and foremost. When you and your twin trigger everything in each other, it can bring about physical, emotional, and mental distress at certain times, so it is important to stay present and true to yourself. Usually, in the twin flame dynamic one twin is more grounded than the other, and the twin will mirror that as well when one of you is not grounded. It just takes time and a routine that works for you to help you to stay grounded. Staying grounded, being pure in thoughts, journaling and being creative, connecting in nature, drinking plenty of water, and taking salt baths will surely help you to feel grounded. One twin will reflect through mirror work how you are not grounded and in which ways you are giving your power away. Through the mirror work, you and your twin will stir each other up to go deeper within. You and your twin flame are a mirror of what you fear and simultaneously desire the most in your own inner healing work.

It is important to remember, as you are going through the mirror exercise, twin flames do not complete you. You are already complete at a soul level. We, instead, complement one another and help each other to grow and become the better versions of ourselves and we don't need anyone outside ourselves to complete us either. I give a perfect example of how I felt my world was caving in and I could not see the light. I wanted desperately to reach out to have my twin help me through what was triggering me in the physical, but God gave me the choice to sit and heal what I had been suppressing or dealing with in a codependent way. God helped me work through my upsets. We can do this. Automatically when we are going through something, we tend to want to reach outside of ourselves because the pain and emotions are so overwhelming that we either choose not to heal this right away or we reach for our twin, and our twin is always with us whether they are physically there or not. It showed and mirrored back to me, through God and my twin, that I am capable of sitting with my emotions and not reaching outside of myself as it is so absolutely hard to sit with your emotions especially when you are used to suppressing them for so long as I did for the last thirty years. This is why it is vital to do the mirror work as it is so important to do the inner work to help connect us back to ourselves and work towards our greatest goals and desires.

Through the mirror work, twin flames help one another find their light side as opposed to their dark side. I realized this in my own union with my twin flame over the weekend of my twin's birthday. I really wanted to see my twin, but I was sick with a migraine. I know we are always connected to one another, but I realized through this experience that I needed to take care of myself and trust that we are there for one another regardless of any situation. The day after my twin's birthday, I realized how much I suppressed my feelings for my twin as I was surrendering myself. This is an important aspect of the twin flame journey. My soul was sobbing and I realized I really wanted to be with my twin as there were lots of fears that got in the way, and the more my soul was screaming out, the more I realized how much I was running from my true feelings. You just need to learn to quiet your mind and the opinions around you as it is *your* life. If you come from a place where people think they have to make every decision for you, remember they do not, as you are more than capable to create the life you want. I realized I was still caught in the thoughts of old programming. The old programming cannot survive in a twin flame reunion. We need to be who we came here to be by letting go of limiting beliefs and not letting others affect us on our path to a union with God, with ourselves, and with our twin flame. Even a small simple email or talking to our twin flame can trigger how we have not been true to ourselves. My twin sent me a song telepathically by Elton John, "I Guess That's Why They Call

It the Blues," to remind me that even through our separation, we are one with each other and that he knows too well through the mirror work that I have a tendency to suppress my feelings for him. He knows that we are always a part of one another, and I am especially reminded of this while I work on releasing what no longer serves me as the old patterns cannot be present in the twin flame dynamic.

The weekend of my twin's birthday, both he and my son's dad showed me through the mirror work where I am hiding behind a safety net. I realize that hiding is causing more anger and upset with myself as I know how many feelings and love I have for God, for myself, and for my twin flame. Therefore, not letting go of what no longer is serving you is not being kind to yourself or to your twin, as you both reflect that onto each other. We tend to retreat to safety from our old programming, as we were taught when we were young that we had to live by certain conditions. Living by old conditions is not a healthy way to live, as deep down inside we know that our twins are the ones we want to have a life with. If we continue not being our true selves, it prolongs the avoidance of a union with God, yourself, and your twin. This journey will be mirrored completely as you and your twin are the brightest mirrors for one another. We reflect all the deep-seated layers that are within each of us. The mirror work shows you where you are hiding your dark parts and where you need to pay attention to yourself. It also shows where you shut down your true feelings. The mirror work shows where you are avoiding your feelings of shame and insecurity. The mirror work shows where you are numbing out and where you need to know how to balance your feminine and masculine energies. Through the mirror work, we tend to want our twins right there as we purge. When we were growing up, we were taught that it was easy to reach outside of ourselves for help. Through the mirror work, you are allowed to purge emotions and sit with them by going within to let go of any and all emotions from the past and moving forward on your path. At times as the energies can be intense and we purge some heavy dark energies, it feels like a death, and you just want to get out from under your emotions. Several times there were moments I wanted to reach out to my twin, but I knew that he would just mirror back to me my own emotions, and I would have to further sit in the junk until I looked at it to heal and forgive myself and move on from things in the past. It may be an awful feeling, like you want to just throw in the towel, as it is a result of our being brought up to be dependent on others for our happiness. We are not taught to sit with our emotions; instead, we are conditioned to sweep them under the rug, to not look at them, in hopes that the feelings or emotions will go away.

In doing the mirror work, even though our twins are our mirror and reflection, our family and friends as well show us where we are holding on in order to feel in control. This happened to me over the weekend when I was filling out some paperwork. My sister was there, and she kept taking control over this simple activity. This moment showed me more of the mirror work I needed in order to heal. She was reflecting back to me where I needed to let go of control. On this journey, particularly when you are working through the mirror work, people and especially your twin will show you where you are holding on to too much control. When working through mirror work, all your dark shadows will surface. As I mentioned earlier in the chapter, our twins are our brightest reflection. When one of us has not healed any of the dark parts, it will reflect back to our twin and vice versa. Be sure to honor and love yourself fully when you are purging and releasing because the more gentle you can be with yourself, the more you can start showing up for yourself and for your twin. When doing the mirror work, in actuality, your twin is your perfect mirror when you are not showing up for yourself and not facing the confidence and abandonment issues that you have not dealt with throughout life.

Throughout the mirror work the more you resist the transition of healing, the more painful and heavy the journey is and feels. Take it one step at a time. The more you are kind to yourself, the more you are kind to your twin. If all you can do is get up and get dressed, then honor that. We live in a world in which we must have a to-do list as my mom would say and then if we do not complete the to-do list, we are hard on ourselves as our twins will mirror that right back. Some days are tougher than others, and it is important not to judge yourself for where you are or how you are feeling. Instead, through the mirror work, meet and embrace yourself where you are.

As they say, "Rome was not built in a day," and eventually you and your twin will heal all aspects of yourselves fully, as you and your twin are the reflection of each other. So, if you seek anything outside of yourself, then you and your twin will constantly reflect this. You or your twin may be keeping each other in the dark, so through your shadow work, you need to be able to sit with feelings and emotions and heal them as there is nothing or anyone who can fix it except you and your twin. We are taught through life that it is better to suppress feelings and reach outside of ourselves for others to heal us, resulting in addictive and negative behaviors, just to further ignore what actually needs to be confronted and healed. Mirror work takes lots of energy work, so make sure you go to the doctor when you are feeling off as you are releasing a lot of emotions and you have to take care of every part of yourself, including your physical and mental health and overall well-being.

CHAPTER 3

Twin Flame Ascension

What is twin flame ascension? Twin flame ascension is the energetic process of remembering our soul self, and releasing anything that is out of resonance with our true authentic self and path. Twin flame ascension also means rising up and becoming a better version of yourself. When you and your twin trigger each other severely at times, it is meant for your souls' growth. As you grow and make major shifts on the twin flame journey, you are using a lot of energy. When you are letting go of limiting beliefs that are no longer in alignment with your soul self, you will feel a lot of these triggers. You must not let triggers from the past weigh you down, so you can move forward with your true authentic self. The release is a necessary process since in order to ascend and to become the best version of ourselves, we cannot hold on to anything from the past that is weighing us down. Every time we go through ascension, we may think it will last forever, and we may ask God and ourselves when will we see the light at the end of the tunnel. As I was writing this chapter, I heard a song called, "This Little Light of Mine." It reminded me that the more we twin flames work through letting go of limiting beliefs and work through triggers effectively to finally see the light at the end of the tunnel, the more we will shine that light out to ourselves and to the rest of the world. The more we consistently work through our blocks to attain the highest and best spiritual life for ourselves, the more we will affect the change that is overdue in this society.

Lots of twin flames work through lots of triggers that can be heart-wrenching at times and to push through something is okay, just as long as you are ready to own it, clear it, and move on. On the twin flame journey and ascension path we must learn, first and foremost, to forgive ourselves, so we can ascend higher. On the twin flame ascension path we are guided to be able to feel our feelings that have been buried down from lifetime to lifetime and to be kind and gentle with ourselves. We can experience our feelings along this path, instead of shoving everything under the rug as we are taught by society that it is not okay to feel love, sadness, or emotions of any kind. We are taught that we have to portray ourselves as superheroes instead of allowing ourselves to become vulnerable. Being vulnerable throughout the twin flame journey is constant even when we would rather hide in our safe cave and come out when we believe it is safe to do so. Once you start feeling your feelings and true soul self, no one has the right or the power to make you think or act differently as you know in your soul what you truly desire and want. All too often we stay stuck in our egos as that is the safest place for us to be, and we ignore our intuition and our soul's calling.

As I mentioned in Chapter 1, thirty years ago I was driving down the highway in the town I grew up in and I heard the words, "You have to write a book." At the time when I heard these words, it was so loud and clear that I thought I was dreaming. Two years after I met my twin who looks like my soulmate who I met thirty years ago, I heard the calling again and saw a clear vision of the title of this book. So, through the twin flame ascension you will be presented with the choice of whether you will stay stuck and stagnant or whether you will heed the call to serve God. As you go through ascension, there may be physical symptoms that are similar to the flu as you clear the old programming that has been stagnant. These may include headaches, feeling as if you are under a pressure cooker, crying at the drop of a hat, and anger, all a result of the fact that you were formerly not able to express your emotions as you had to repress them. You may also feel physical pain as your joints in all areas in your body are recalibrating while you are getting rid of old unwanted energy and bringing in and anchoring the new you. At times you feel very nauseous as you are working on standing in power and not giving your power away. As a society, we are so used to giving our power away that when we are learning to stand on our own, we experience nausea and other physical ailments at times as we are clearing and learning to stand in our power and not let people dull our shine.

Indeed, at times you may experience unexpected aches and pains. When I first met my twin, I experienced frozen shoulder, an acute condition of pain and stiffness in the shoulder joint. As twins are connected in heart space, if one twin is shouldering lots of responsibility, the other twin can feel it especially through the ascension process. Twins may feel deep depression or anxiety as twins are connected through both the heart and eyes, and if one twin is going through anxiety or depression, the other can feel it as well. When you meet your twin flame, you go through an ascension process. While going through the ascension process, it feels like the process is never ending, but it is a necessity to clear all blocks and feel your feelings and let them out in emotional and physical ways. Ascension is also considered the act of rising to a higher consciousness level, as you are beginning to vibrate at a higher level of consciousness. Just know when you are going through this that you are not going crazy or suffering something psychological. The old patterns, behaviors, and beliefs are all being pushed to the surface to heal as the old you cannot thrive in a twin flame relationship and spiritual awakening. At times you may feel a bit disoriented as you are leaving the beliefs that you thought you knew behind.

When you are ascending higher, you basically are connecting to God, angels, and other spiritual realms. When you experience unusual aches and pains as mentioned earlier in this chapter, you are releasing the old that is no longer serving you for your soul's growth. You are purifying and releasing blocked energy that eventually can no longer exist in the new paradigm. At times you may experience spiritual fatigue, which I have experienced from time to time. You know you want to rise up as part of your soul's growth, but on a human level we tend to work and push too much, and at times on the ascension path you need to take a step back and be still. Our human side wants all the answers here and now instead of allowing the flow of energy and being still to put you in your intuitive space, a place where you will discover steps to follow for your highest path.

All too often when you meet your twin, you want on a human side to hurry and heal the old paradigm, but through the twin flame ascension path we must be patient and have lots of wisdom to heal the old because if you heal too fast, you will feel that you are under a pressure cooker and that you are experiencing what feels like a psychological breakdown, so it is best to step away and take care of yourself as self-care on the twin flame ascension path is a necessity and one that needs to be incorporated into your daily life. Our will and determination are an integral part of the acceptance that we must allow our individual twin flame counterparts to achieve his or her own spiritual growth and level of consciousness. Most will come to their own understanding of the spiritual concepts of the twin flame ascension at their own pace through experiences and insights. Twin flames will travel many different paths sometimes through harsh lessons before the ascension process and spiritual awakening occurs. We must remember that everyone is ascending at a different pace, and everyone is walking his or her own unique path as individual sparks of the one creator of God.

We individuals who are on the spiritual path to enlightenment progress in ways and can ascend at different degrees and different levels. I cannot reiterate enough that during our soul's growth we give our twin the space to heal and not to pressure him or her as, in turn, we are pressuring ourselves. As I mentioned in Chapter 2, we twins are the brightest reflection to one another. Since we are also having a human experience as well as going through a spiritual awakening and ascending higher, we must make sure we do not judge ourselves, our twins, and others too harshly. As you go through the twin flame ascension process, you are in the process of dismantling your ego little by little to honor your soul's truth.

As I stated earlier, we as a society live in fear and worry. The ascension process is the process in which we are letting go of our old self and dysfunctional programming that was instilled in us when we were growing up. The old paradigm must go to be able to open up to the new paradigm and the new you. Through the twin flame ascension process, especially in the beginning and throughout the journey, you are always purging and releasing. As I already mentioned, the release may come in many form, as your soul starts screaming at you to wake up and become your true authentic self. We tend as a society to run from our fears rather than face our fears or shadow self. We tend to hide at times when we are purging huge amounts of fear, guilt, shame, and anger as we do not want to face ourselves, our twins, and others because it can feel vulnerable once your twin, especially, sees the raw side of you. Through the ascension process we are breaking codependent patterns. By this I mean as co-dependency cannot survive in a twin flame journey. We are awakening from the past as our society has suffered years of abusive relationships; therefore, whether physically or mentally you need to learn to break the cycle of abuse through the ascension process. We are all worthy of becoming our best versions of ourselves and achieving what we came here to accomplish, and no one has the right to take away your right to learn life lessons which will make you become a stronger you. This is why the twin flame ascension process is absolutely difficult, and, from time to time, you can experience spiritual fatigue as you are letting go of cycles of abuse and co-dependency. Through the twin flame ascending higher and higher, the purging process feels like everything you thought you ever knew is wreaking havoc and you are opening your eyes to it.

As I mentioned in Chapter 1, when I looked into my twin's eyes in the meeting room, he opened my eyes to the fact that I was worth a lot more than I believed as I was living my life. At times when the purging is intense and overwhelming, in reality you know in your heart and soul that you need to persevere in order to become the best version of yourself. Sometimes we must go through these overwhelming emotions and uncomfortable purges to ascend higher on the twin flame journey or spiritual path to enlightenment. Through the ascension process we realize that we can learn to trust in ourselves and that we do not have to seek answers outside of ourselves. As you purge the process of being codependent, you will experience deep healing as it is necessary to release attachment and co-dependency. I know before meeting my twin flame, I never felt that I had lived my full authentic life. I kept running from my true feelings, living my life through the lens of someone else instead of making the best core choices for myself to live. When I met my twin flame, it opened me and awakened me to more ways to know and become the person I am meant to be instead of hiding under a rock or in my favorite cave or behind a mask for the rest of my life. The struggles that we twin flames have experienced through life will be pushed to the surface to face and heal in order to become better version of ourselves. As the purges get so intense through the ascension process there will be times that we just want to blame our twin and anyone around us as we are purging heavy core issues. We must remember that the process is only shining the light on the healing you need to do in order to heal the beliefs of people that thought we were not capable of being a certain way. We heal the belief that other people's thoughts can dictate how we should be and how we should live. We are always perfect but when upheaving massive amounts of core issues, at times you may not feel you are perfect but you are

This is why it is so important to honor ourselves on a daily basis as we are purging heavy programming that was attached to us as a child and that we lived through in our teenage and adult life, only to be able to be pushed to the surface when our spiritual awakening began once we met our twin flame. At times this is why when we are healing lots of heavy emotions through the ascension process, we are always continuing self-care and being conscious of not beating ourselves up when we want a certain answer. We just need to allow the process to unfold and be present to be able to walk our path as we are so used to having someone dictate how our lives should be lived. Just be kind to yourself and if you need to take time for yourself, it is not selfish to honor yourself as you are purging lots of old belief systems that have been placed on us and to unlearn all the negative self-talk and all the negative programming placed on us.

Trust me, there are days when you want to throw in the towel, but the more you heal lots of old programming the better as it will benefit you, your twin, and those around you. We twins are here to bring more positive light to the Earth and let go of old belief systems that simply do not and will not work. Ultimately, it is God who makes the decisions of how he wants us to create our lives, but as we were growing up we were taught to be codependent and listen to people who thought they knew better for us when, literally, we have the answers within us and it is our life to live for ourselves and not for others. Once we can purge this false belief, our eyes are open to so much more when we see that we were so closed off and not living our full truth and potential. At times when you are purging intense emotions, you may feel as though you have taken a step back from progressing forward. Know that you may be but that you have to feel your emotions to heal them in order for there to be forward movement. There are times throughout the ascension process that you feel that the healing feels like an eternity, but in reality we must bring to the surface what is not in resonance with ourselves and with our life's purpose. I always knew that I needed to write this book, and, as I mentioned earlier, when you do not listen, God and your angels will literally bring the message around again when you are ready.

Since we are living a human experience as well as working and living our soul's journey, we must not beat ourselves up when the answer is not clear. We as a society have often been used to living in a logical state of mind and when someone or a twin flame comes in to spark that catalytic heart awakening, we must be gentle with ourselves as we are in the process of evolving. Through the twin flame ascension process, always feel free to reach out for support as this journey is not for the faint of heart and things should be taken neither too lightly nor too seriously. We must find balance with the soul and human side of our growth. There were many times I wanted to throw in the towel on this journey only to find that it was my ego fighting me. I needed to know how not to pressure myself for all the answers as that was my old human side wanting to take control and find all the answers at once. The answers to your soul's journey will be given to you a little at a time and not all at once. If we were shown all the answers and were able to achieve perfection, there would be no room to grow and if all our answers were presented all at once to us, we may become overwhelmed and have a psychological break down, so it is better to tackle our journey in phases.

Just remember that you are not alone on this journey although it sometimes feels like you are, but that is an illusion and that there is always support on the twin flame journey, especially when you are going through intense ascension energies. Remember that Jesus gave his life for us and in a way we are finding our way to be selfless and bring more light to Earth as the programming that once existed thirty to forty years ago will not be tolerated moving forward as people are here to seek the truth and live in truth rather than be manipulated and controlled by the benefit of others. We are sovereign beings who deserve to have the life we want and not let others decide what our life will be like as God is the one in control on this journey and any journey that we are embarking on.

While purging through the ascension process, we must learn lots of self-care and understand that we have all the answers within us despite the fact that we were taught differently, so be kind to yourself first and foremost. Part of self-care is eating healthy foods, and as we ascend higher and higher, it is a necessity that we learn to eat healthier when we are stressed or we will not nourish ourselves properly. Eating clean and nutritious food as much as you can will help you further your ascension journey, especially to release all the toxins in your body which will allow pure love and light into your body. Furthermore, drinking water with lemon or cucumber will help purify you as you purge when you are purging heavy intense energies on the ascension path to enlightenment. Connecting in nature will help as well as you learn to just be out in nature and not feel the rush and pressure society puts on each one of us, a pressure that makes us feel as if we need to have all the answers or be the perfect person. We are already perfect, but often, on this journey, we find ourselves putting lots of pressure on ourselves to get immediate answers instead of quieting the mind and learning to feel at peace with ourselves. This is another false programming we are releasing as we as human beings learn to live in logic and not allow ourselves to be pushed for answers. So, connecting with nature will help significantly as you ground your energies. We are all one and connected to everything especially nature.

You will eventually feel so much lighter and peaceful once you let go of all negative belief systems that have been placed on us throughout our lives. Through the ascension process we are learning to clear bloodlines through ancestors as what we once knew through our grandparents and parents cannot exist in a new paradigm and a new you. Ascension is not a single day process. It is a long journey that takes time to help mold you in many ways. We on our human side are so used to wanting everything now as society is always about the answers in the here in now instead of progressing a little at a time. During the ascension process we are meant to take a pause and be still and listen to the next step of our ascension path. If we rush the ascension process because we want to know all the answers all at once, we must stop and remember that this can only be achieved a little at a time. Only the divine source and God will give you the answers to your ascension path a little at a time.

During the ascension process both twins work as the light for the other and show the right path that leads toward forever happiness. Through this ascension stage of ascension both twins have gone through tough stages in which our souls have to decide what is right and what is wrong. This is something that cannot be achieved overnight as this occurs over many months or years until your soul is ready to become purified with your higher self and your twin's higher self. Remember as you go through the ascension process, it is a constant experience of peeling back layers upon layers of the old you in order to become the new you. Remember who you were meant to be here on Earth and do not continue living in the lens of someone or something else. This is a journey that takes time and it is all about God, you, and your twin and what you came here to achieve on this Earth. So, remember to be gentle with yourself through every step on the ascension path, which is the path to enlightenment.

CHAPTER 4

Music

Twin Flames share a telepathic connection, especially through music. As I mentioned in Chapter 1, we often ignore the soul song urge to which God and our soul are guiding us as we are so used to living in our comfort zone and our protective safe space when in actuality God is leading us back to our soul's truth. This is what happened to me from the time my son was born. As previously mentioned, I was being led back to meeting my twin flame who was my son's preschool teacher. Years before meeting my twin flame in the physical, God and my soul would push me to go grocery shopping in my twin flame's neighborhood or to look for a house to buy which would have been a block away from where my twin currently lives, something I did not know at the time. There were mysterious forces guiding me.

Now back to the music of this chapter. A few years into meeting my twin flame he told me that he had been the music director for twenty years at Saint Joseph's Church in Belmont, Massachusetts. The priest of the church where my twin flame Charley was the organ director was a family friend named Thomas Mahoney. Thomas Mahoney would pray with my dad on occasion during his cancer treatment. As they say, you should always follow your heart and soul, but in today's society we live in so much fear to move or live in the zone of comfort or familiarity. As I mentioned, God and my soul were guiding me to my twin flame long before I met him in the physical. I would always take my son to church when he was a baby. We were living in Needham, Massachusetts, and I would take him to two churches there: Saint Joseph's Church and

Saint Bartholomew Church. Ultimately, I would end up taking him to Saint Bartholomew, where a few years into meeting my twin flame he mentioned that he would play the organ on occasion at mass there. In addition, I would take my son to Sacred Heart Church in Newton, Massachusetts, where my twin Charley would also play on occasion. However, it was mostly to Saint Bartholomew Church that I would take my son, not even realizing my twin played there, but my soul was guiding me all along to meet him.

Twin flames share the same soul DNA and agree to meet in this life at some point. At times, or most of the time, twin flames live parallel lives frequenting many of the same places until they are ready to meet in the physical. I know my twin and I share the love of music as I used to work for Strawberries Music Store when I started out in the Watertown, Massachusetts location. I mention Watertown is where I started working at Strawberries Music because, as I mentioned in my previous chapter, twin flames share a soul DNA since the time they are born. I also mentioned previously my twin and I have always worked or lived close to each other for the last thirty years. It is part of the soul plan that my twin lived in Cambridge, Massachusetts at the time and Cambridge and Watertown are neighboring towns. In fact, as I was writing this music chapter, my twin flame's higher self sent me a song by Kenny Rogers and Dolly Parton called "Islands in the Stream," reminding me of our connection and how even though we are not physically together as of yet, we are always there for one another despite how things seem on the outside. Through my experience of my telepathic communication with my twin, I know that music is a large part of the spiritual connection between us; music is an important part of our communication, as it is for other twin flames I have met on this journey. It helps to recognize this, especially when we tend to have fears and doubts that creep into our thoughts from time to time.

We twins are here to bring pure love to this Earth despite the challenges that get in the way of twins coming together in this lifetime. As I mentioned, twins live parallel lives or frequent the same places or streets. For example, I lived on Webster Street in Needham, Massachusetts and years before my twin worked at the high school on Webster Street in Needham. He also lived parallel to Garden Street in Cambridge, Massachusetts and I grew up on Garden Road in Wellesley, Massachusetts. Further, regarding the same name churches as I mentioned my twin Charley was the organ director at Saint Joseph's Church in Belmont and their affiliate church in Watertown, Massachusetts is Saint Luke's. Coincidentally, I was baptized at Saint Luke's Church in Lakewood, Ohio. I attended mass at Saint Luke's in Lakewood, Ohio, and as a small girl my mom would always tell me I would sing along with the choir even though I did not know many of the words at that time.

This makes sense as twins are always connected, and my twin has always played the organ at church. As a part of this music chapter, I wanted to include the song "Speechless," by Dan and Shay as this describes when I met my twin and how I could feel something different for my twin than for any other person. Twin flames express themselves to each another in words, subtle expressions, and telepathy. Every time I listen to this song, the lyrics ring true to describe the connection my twin and I have for one another. Have you ever had that feeling with your twin flame? Twin flames speak to one another through music, like when the music of your twin flame connection suddenly plays on the radio or you cannot get a certain song out of your head. I know that my twin flame and I speak to each other through music as is also the case with so many twin flames that I have encountered on this path.

Telepathy is one of the strongest ways that twin flames communicate and have a strong connection with one another when they are not yet physically together. Sometimes even when twin flames are physically together, telepathy is a strong connection especially through music. Music is a powerful way for twin flames to communicate. The music we send to one another is inherently spiritual but it also carries a powerful electromagnetic energy. Twin flames carry a lot of emotions in their emotional body where they have had blockages from one lifetime to another. These emotional blocks can prevent true flames from expressing their true nature. After being knocked down by negative outside influences and being made to feel that they are not worthy, twin flames carry that blockage in their emotional body. When they activate one another through the heart chakra and kundalini awakening, then lots of telepathy occurs especially through music. One example is when

I had a video made for the retirement of my twin flame Charley, and one of the songs I put in the video was "Forever Young," by Rod Stewart. Some of the following lyrics represented the connection we have.

May the good lord be with you
down every road you roam.
And may sunshine and happiness
surround you when you're far from home.
And may you grow to be proud
Be courageous and be brave.
And in my heart you will remain
Forever young, forever young, forever young yeah!!

As I was writing the lyrics of the song, I realized that when adding this song in Charley's retirement video, I chose a song which is definitely an example of the theme of twin flames. It makes sense that I put "Forever Young" in the video as it signifies that through our journey together when twin flames have been apart, we must always follow the guiding light and intuition on days when we want to connect to one another. This song also reminds me of how my twin and all twin flames share a oneness. Today, I am reminded that when twins are connected, they are always using their guiding light and intuition to help guide each other throughout life and to come back to meet in this life at some point. As I was writing the lyrics of "Forever Young," I remembered that earlier I was in my car and a firefly was flying around my car. The spiritual meaning of the firefly is to always follow your guiding light and your intuition. The spiritual significance of the firefly relates as well to Rod Stewart's song, and it reminds me of the connection between twin flames and the next steps twin flames take to embark on this journey to oneness and unconditional love.

Today, while writing the music chapter, I received a song sent to me titled, "We Are," by Kari Jobe. This song reminded me that on the twin flame journey when you are connected to your twin, you both meet one another in darkness, as we are here to bring more light to the Earth we live in. Also, to completely shine our light, to love unconditionally ourselves, our twin flames, and the world around us. The song reminded me as well not to hide and stay small but to completely shine our light as the world needs to know that it is not okay to put conditions on one another. The song reminds us that it is important to live a peace-filled, authentic life that we may choose for ourselves and to be accepting of what we choose.

A few weeks ago, I went to church and at mass they played a hymn called In Every Age and it was about hope. The sermon piggy-backed on this song that we are the light and hope and that we are here to make changes within ourselves so that we can love one another as we love ourselves. If we do not have love for ourselves, then how can we have love for our twin flame or the whole world at large? It is not to say that we have to be friends with everyone and always be compassionate with the world at large. I believe the song "In Every Age" strikes a chord in me as I am embarking on this journey, and it reminds me that this world needs more love, light, and hope, rather than a world filled with judgment and criticism. We must remember that our soul is guiding us each day to live our mission and to be able to walk our path with truth and authenticity. We as a society have been brought up in so much fear, and we must learn to let go of fear and live the life we are meant to live and continually embrace love, peace and hope each day. We also need not to conform to anyone or anything that is out of alignment with our soul being. This is the spiritual work of our individual path and the journey of twin flames.

Twin Flames share music through telepathic communication in order to share messages and emotions. While twin flames are in physical separation from one another, the telepathy between twins through music helps to strengthen their connection and guide the next steps to embark on, as well as reminding the twin flames how the connection runs on a deep soul level and how the bond between them can never be broken no matter what. Whether we are physically together with our twin flame or not, we recognize our twin flame's energy through our soul song energy. Throughout any separation with your twin flame, music enhances your ability to communicate on all levels with your twin from 5D to 3D communication. This communication helps you trust one another where trust was formerly lacking for each of you and allows you to be able to trust that union will happen within each of you individually and together in oneness. At times when you want to relay a message telepathically through music to your twin, it is the best way as it helps each of you work through blocks of communication and resistance when you want to hold onto an emotion from the past, but you need to let it go, to be able to be vulnerable, and to not hide behind a mask, thus becoming your true authentic self. Music calms the heart and mind which plays an important part of the twin flame communication as you and your twin have a unique and deep connection on a soul level and when one of you is out of balance, the other can feel it quite literally. Music helps ground your thoughts and actions as the twin flame journey is not for the faint of heart, but it is rather a journey which requires you to open your eyes to see where truth has been hidden from you all along and to become into soul alignment with your soul song frequency. Believing and knowing that you and your twin flame are sending one another music through telepathy requires a lot of faith and trust in yourself and in one another, especially at times when you feel doubt creep in when in actuality you are hearing correctly. Your twin and you will send music and other signs and synchronicities to one another, so whenever you hear a song that your twin flame sends you or vice versa, it is a chance to go within and communicate and build trust with one another. God and your spirit guides are always here to confirm that you are on the right path and should continue with your authentic and soul song truth.

Another song that is significant on the journey with my twin flame is "Landslide," by Fleetwood Mac. This song is significant as when we twin flames meet each other, we are connected on a deep soul connection, and we see one another's reflection as we have to heal our shadow side individually. Do you want to explain the meaning of shadow side? If you have not healed your shadow side that you have been hiding behind, the song "Landslide" will continually play through telepathy for both you and your twin until you have healed what needs to be healed. A song also that my twin plays on the organ at church is "On Eagles' Wings." This song came to me in a difficult moment as well, as I mentioned that at times the twin flame journey can be heart-wrenching and not for the faint of heart. I feel "On

Eagles' Wings" demonstrates how when we are releasing the past to become present on this journey and mission with our twin, God is holding us in his palm, and when we are letting go of the past, we must remain strong and not have fear as he is holding our hand every step of the way as we rise and evolve. Additionally, you can find the beauty in everything along the soul song journey. One song as well that resonates with this chapter about music and twin flame journey is Fragrance Prayer, by Tom Booth. The words are as follows:

> *Dear Jesus, help me to spread your fragrance everywhere that I go.*
>
> *Dear Jesus, flood my soul with your spirit and your love.*
>
> *Shine through me and be so in me that every soul that I come in contact with may feel your presence in my soul.*
>
> *Stay with me and then I shall begin to shine as you shine so to shine as a light to all.*

This prayer I was guided to listen to when I first realized and understood that there was a connection with my twin flame and me. The lyrics of the prayer Dear Jesus make sense as they remind me of twin flames meeting in this lifetime to come into mission with one another and to spread love on this Earth. The words remind me not to be in fear of Jesus as he gave his life for us and we are God's children, so we are here to carry on the message of oneness that we are not separate from one another, and no one individual needs to put anyone above the other as we are all equals. We are reminded as well that we are the beacons of light spreading more love and light to the Earth and that we do the work of Jesus by shining our light no matter what, just like he did for us. We all have a purpose to love and to shine our light onto ourselves and to spread the light to others wherever and whenever we are needed. The prayer reminds as well not to be afraid to let Jesus shine through you, so you can help heal the world at large and not be afraid to go within and listen to his words and to understand how you can help to heal the world. One other song that resonates with this twin flame connection is the song my friend Chad LaMarsh sings, "Just Remember." The words are as follows:

I'll do my best to bring a smile to your day.
I'll say the things to make your worries fade away.
Create a calming for your peace of mind
It's all for you and you are mine

Just remember I will be your friend
I'll catch you if you fall
I'm your biggest fan
It's all for you, only you

There will be times when we're further from near
but we can hold the memories of our greatest times
we're not always in the moment holding hands side by side
But you're always in my soul, you hold my heart within your life
Just remember, that I love you
Let me share within these moments, breathe the golden air
Just remember, no need to be afraid
I'm never far behind, I'll never turn away
It's all for you

You're the sunshine of each moment
You gave a reason for each day
You elevate the life condition
for everyone that looks your way
Don't surrender to the places
where you hide within your heart
On a pedestal I see you, like a perfect work of art

Whatever you are needing
wherever you may be
Just remember that I'm here
I'll be the air that you can breathe

Just remember I will be your friend
I'll catch you if you fall, I'm your biggest fan
Just remember, that I love you
Let us share within these moments, share within these moments
Let us share within these moments, It's all for you only you.
All for you
Just remember, just remember, just remember

I feel the song "Just Remember" signifies the soul love that twin flames share no matter the distance or the stage at which the twin flames find themselves working toward union with self and harmonious union with one another. Twin flames are always within one another as I mentioned in previous chapters; twin flames share the same soul with two different bodies that express their unique gifts. Your twin is you, you and your twin are perfect counterparts, and you and your twin help guide each other when you ultimately meet in the physical. You have been guiding one another long before you have met, as you have shared the same soul DNA since the time you were born as you have agreed to meet in this life.

CHAPTER 5

Synchronicities

As I started writing Chapter 5, I was reminded of how many astounding synchronicities are encountered on the twin flame journey. I am writing this as my twin and I share a life path number 4 and his birthday is 4/6. I often see license plate numbers especially reminding me of our unique connection through the number 4 and of what I came here on Earth to accomplish. My twin and I are also the second to the last sibling in our families. He is the 9th child in his family and I am the 6th child in my family. Thus, when you go in doubt on this twin flame journey and wonder if what you are experiencing is real or all in your head, then you will get synchronicities that remind you that your experience is real and you are not going crazy!

As I mentioned in previous chapters, at times when you have sporadic communication with your twin, then your logic mind starts to get in the way. I do not really like to limit our connection as twin flames by labeling it, but I do this as it is the title and the subject of my book. If you are wondering if this is a real connection, it definitely is. One day I was in line waiting for something and I heard the number 78 and the color blue. My spirit guides were reminding me of my deep connection to my twin flame. We have the number 78 in common. That is when my twin graduated from college and when I had a near-death experience, so we were transitioning into a new life with twists and turns. My near-death experience happened literally right down the street from where he currently lives, but at the time he was not living there as he graduated from college in 1978 from Catholic University in Washington, D.C. that year. I was trying to figure out the color blue, and then months into the journey, I noticed that he drives a blue car. Another synchronicity is that my twin was born in 1956 and my Dad graduated from college in 1956. I find this to be a synchronicity as these two men, besides God, have been a significant driving force in my life.

I am forever grateful everyday as a lot of synchronicities can be astounding on this journey, but they happen to remind you of what you came here on Earth to accomplish. As I mentioned in a previous chapter, a beautiful synchronicity that my twin and I have is the love for music. As this is a chapter of synchronicities, I do not want to go too much in depth about the connection with music, but I will let you know that whenever you doubt this connection, look no further as your guides will let you know that you are not dreaming and that the twin flame connection is real. Another synchronicity is that my twin received his master's degree in education and as a part of his degree he studied psychology. I, too, went to school for psychology and sociology and at one point was considering a career working with young children with special needs. Ultimately, my twin taught young children some of whom had special needs. I worked with children, as well, at one point and I actually volunteer on occasion at a place called Birthday Wishes to provide birthday parties for kids who are less fortunate. My twin also provided a Christmas at his house for orphaned children who would not otherwise be able to celebrate Christmas.

The summer of 2016 when I discovered we were twin flames, I was sitting outside on my front steps and saw at least six red cardinals in my yard. I was in awe and could not figure out why so many cardinals would be in my yard. Two years into our meeting I had traveled to Washington D. C. to write part of my book and decided I would take a tour of the campus of Catholic University. Something led me to the bookstore, and what is their mascot but a red cardinal! That was another synchronicity on this journey. Not only were the cardinals in my yard on that day, but it was also the night of the Paul McCartney concert, where my friend and I were going, and literally out of the entire venue at Fenway Park, where the concert was held, there was a teacher assistant who taught in my twin's classroom sitting behind my friend and me at the concert. It was the universe's way of saying how deep the connection is between my twin flame and me, but at the time of these synchronicities your logic mind is trying to comprehend everything. Literally, you cannot use your logic mind in the twin flame connection, or if you do what I did when my twin and I first parted ways after school ended, you may feel you are going crazy or you are having a psychological breakdown. Trust me - you are not. These thoughts and feelings in your mind are why it is so important to get as much support as possible on this journey as there are so many people nowadays meeting their twin flames. As I already mentioned, you do not go looking for your twin flame, rather he or she will appear and basically turn your world upside down. As I mentioned in previous chapters, my twin and I lived and worked close to each other for the last thirty years and met in the physical when my son had him as his preschool teacher.

Another example of the synchronicities in the twin flame journey is something that happened recently at a car dealership. My son and I were looking to buy a car for me and my son wanted to go and chat with the other sales people at the dealership, and literally I stopped for a second as one of the salesmen whom we were working with said, "Oh, you want to meet so and so." This person happened to have the same name as my twin. Therefore, any time you are in doubt on this journey, God and the universe will remind you that you are on the right path. Remember that sometimes our human side wants to fight things, but our soul always knows the way. As I mentioned in a previous chapter, my twin was the organ director of Saint Joseph's Church and their sister Church in Watertown, Massachusetts is Saint Luke's Church and I was baptized at Saint Luke's in Lakewood, Ohio.

The other day I saw my twin walking as I was driving my son to a dental appointment and my guides know how much I question everything, so automatically they showed me that I was on the right path and that I was meant to see my twin. To confirm this, the numbers I saw were 46 - my twin's birthday - which I always see and 56 - the year he was born - and 112 which is the room number he taught in. At one point yesterday, before I saw my twin walking, I was hearing a message as I was questioning if I was on the right path. As I have said, I always receive a sign that I am indeed on the right path. Another time, literally on the way to a twin flame conference back in May of 2019 on the way to Plymouth, Massachusetts, I saw a license plate on the way to the event that said "I get it." This was another very clear message that I was on the right path.

Remember that your soul is guiding you on this journey and your soul always knows the answer, even if our human nature wants to fight the ego. You literally need to drop the ego when it comes to this soul love. I have always felt something for my twin and my soul and my human side are always battling it out, but in the end, I just need to listen to my soul guiding me. What I firmly believe is that we as twin flames are always learning from synchronicities on the twin flame journey to not fight with our human ego, even though the majority of us do, as our ego is here to protect us from getting hurt. Synchronicities are here to keep us on our life path as well, as there will be people in our lives who will constantly throw us from our path, and we can either choose to pay attention to the signs or have tunnel vision and not grow or evolve into the person we are meant to be.

Another synchronicity that happened to me recently was when I was listening to a twin flame couple being interviewed, and they were mentioning that birds are significant on this journey as is anything to do with nature. I mentioned the significance of the cardinals but blackbirds have also had a significant impact on this journey with my twin flame and me. I experience not just one blackbird but a flock of blackbirds flying over me a lot of the time. As I was listening to the couple being interviewed and they were mentioning how birds are significant on their journey, all of a sudden, I was driving and a flock of blackbirds flew over my car. The meaning behind the vision of blackbirds is that we must trust our intuition and the unlimited possibilities which are within our reach. Blackbirds teach us to embrace the mystery of the unknown. Blackbirds will appear on your spiritual path as a beacon to know and become the true person you are. It was a great reminder when these birds flocked around my car. Every so often it is natural that we question if we are on the correct path or we may encounter other people who will try to throw us from our path, and it is up to us and nobody else to pick ourselves up and keep finding and discovering who we are in every moment. Blackbirds also help people to follow their intuition and, when something is not quite right, to slow down and connect to their intuition.

I was sitting here remembering the time at the beginning of the twin flame journey when I did not know how I was feeling day to day. I needed to find the right people to talk to, so I started going back to a bereavement group. I knew my mom was not going to be cured of her COPD, so I went to the group just to connect in general. One question I asked God was if I was on the correct journey. Then came the answer. I saw that a member of the group was wearing a sweatshirt with the college name where my twin went: Catholic University. So, I knew I was on the right path as this was another synchronicity in the beginning of my journey.

A song by Alanis Morisette, called "You Learn," came to me as I was writing this chapter. The lyrics are a great reminder that on this journey when we have had an awakening by our twin, we all have experienced how we need to express our emotions in all ways whether positive or negative and learn to love, but it is also okay to cry and scream or be creative as well. Along the path, it important to feel and release all of your emotions. As they say, "You need to feel it to heal it." This song is a great reminder that especially on this path to enlightenment people may want to judge you, but you must just keep going and following your intuition. Throughout the twin flame journey, we should always trust our intuition as we learn along the way that no matter what people say and judge, it is our path to discover who we truly are.

I most recently saw Deepak Chopra on television. The words of Deepak Chopra completely resonated as well with the experiences along the twin flame journey, and I felt his words as a part of the great synchronicity we encounter, especially for many of us who lose faith and trust on this journey. Deepak Chopra was talking about acceptance. I thought that this was another moment of great synchronicity listening to him talk about acceptance. First, we must accept ourselves. He also defines acceptance as not trying to change ourselves or another person. Accept yourself and others as they are. If you try to change another, you disrupt the flow and, for the other person or yourself, you are stopping your growth or someone else's growth. We all came here on Earth to accomplish something and with the twin flame journey, literally, your twin flame turns your world upside down as mine did. The twin flame experience was to awaken my talents and gifts that had been lying dormant within my energy field for so long.

Every day I see another synchronicity which is to continue going within, as within ourselves we have all the answers. I want to write about this journey, as I feel it is important for the newer twin flames to understand because most of our lives we have sought answers outside of ourselves which is an ancestral pattern we need to break in order to move forward to better ourselves. I also wanted to reiterate that we are always connected to our twin through our heart, and, and so anytime you try to use your logic mind you will create confusion within yourself. It takes a lot of time to really still your mind, but I wanted to write this as well to help others find their way differently as we are always taught to use our logic mind. This journey is not about using the logic mind. It can be a constant struggle if you let your mind take over as you will be in constant battle with yourself, so that is why I recommend getting still with yourself and finding out what gifts and talents you can bring to the twin flame dynamic. I felt this was a synchronicity as this has been coming up a lot for me to work through on my journey since it is different for everyone, but as a society we are taught to listen to stay in our logic mind, as that is where the ego protects us, instead of following our heart. Additionally, if you are new to this journey, it is also important to get as much support as you can along the way to stay creative and in your heart space, as this path has many challenges, and we all need to be able to sit with uncomfortable emotions from time to time.

Another synchronicity I experienced this morning before writing this chapter on my way driving my son to school was hearing a song called "Drops of Jupiter" by Train. I felt this song was significant in this chapter as the lyrics talk about finding yourself and asking questions about whether someone misses you while you were off discovering yourself. I feel this song has a message as we twin flames all too often want to be with our twin, and as I said, that can happen as long as we look within and not look for our twin or anyone to save us. We have to learn life lessons by going within as often as possible. As I mentioned earlier, we tend to look externally on the outside rather than on what is on the inside. This journey is all about trusting your intuition and believing in yourself and taking back your personal power.

As I mentioned, we all are connected to God and that God is the person within ourselves. This brings me to a scene from the play, *The Lion King,* in which they sing a verse: *He lives within me.* These lyrics are about how God lives within each of us, and we have the right to better ourselves and trust our instincts. We as a society have been taught not to trust, especially if you have come from an ancestral pattern that does not let you find your true, authentic self and you are living day by day just to get through life. An awakening triggers all that you have not accomplished in this lifetime and helps you find your authentic self through a twin flame or a spiritual awakening.

On this journey your spirit guides and angels will assist you, as well as God, of course, and you will experience the presence of spirit animals. I am reminded of a bird that was presented to me when I first became spiritually awakened by my twin. A bird was up in the tree in my yard. I was in awe of this beautiful bird, a falcon. The other morning, as my son and I were having breakfast, I was again reminded of this bird, so I know and feel this is a big part of the journey as well. The falcon was up in my tree and caught my attention as it was huge, and I had seen huge birds like this many times. I know this is my spirit guide animal come to help guide me on this journey. The falcon symbolizes confidence, bravery, wisdom, skillfulness, spirituality, patience, and independence. My guides and my son were reminding me to keep shining my light and to be constantly brave and confident with myself and my twin. All twin flames always have positive energy and remain positive despite things that may appear different because we are living in our authentic truth.

I wanted to include this part in this section of the synchronicity chapter as my son, my spirit guides, and God were reminding me about the falcon. Therefore, I felt it was an important piece to write about as the falcon was one of the first birds to appear at the beginning of the twin flame journey. The majestic falcon presented itself to me around the time I received the clear vision of the title of my book, *Twin Flames and How They Change Your World.* Another synchronicity was when I went to Hyattsville, Maryland two years after meeting my twin and writing part of my book. I was waiting at the train station for the hotel shuttle to pick me up to bring me to the hotel and the wait was a bit long. I was growing impatient as we humans do, but I decided to keep my patience until the hotel shuttle came.

The driver said, "Oh, so sorry we were late. We had to pick up some other passengers along the way." As I was sitting in the hotel shuttle on my way back to the hotel, I met a family, and the little boy's name happened to be the same name as my twin. The universe and God will remind you through synchronicities, such as meeting people with the same name as your twin, that you are on the right path. Not only did the little boy have the same name as my twin, but so did his father, as well as a friend of theirs who was traveling with them. She said that she also had wanted to give her son the same name as the little boy and the father.

After the long day, I was tired from traveling, and I know it was God's way of saying that I was on the right path. So, the next day, I went out and I asked God to please show me a sign to know whether I should continue my vacation in this place and, literally, I looked up at the sky and saw an infinity symbol in the sky. I thought this unusual symbol in the sky was really cool as I have mentioned earlier, my twin and I share a life path number 4, which then adds up to 8, and the infinity symbol looks like an 8. It was definitely God's way of saying that I was in the right place.

There are many meanings to the infinity symbol. I feel the definition of infinity best describes the twin flame connection as the symbol can be drawn in one continuous movement and has neither a beginning nor an end. It holds with it the ideas of no limitations and infinite possibilities. These beliefs are what I feel this journey is about. We are uniquely and infinitely connected to everyone, especially our twin flame and each one of us is capable of achieving infinite possibilities throughout life. Another meaning of the infinity symbol is that of never-ending unconditional love. It also represents individual empowerment and unconditional love for yourself and your twin in the world around you. This is really what the twin flame connection is: to reach oneness with yourself and your eternal flame, who is always there spiritually even though he or she may not be with you physically and to remember that you are infinite in everything that you do. The infinity symbol reminds me of ideas and experiences I will go over in the next chapter in which I will discuss the red string of fate and the first year into my connection to my twin.

The red string of fate is similar to the infinity symbol as it is a red string that stretches and tangles but never breaks. The meaning behind the red string of fate is that the two people connected by the red string of fate are destined lovers, regardless of place, time, or circumstances. This magical cord may stretch or tangle, but it will never break. The red string is similar in concept to the infinity symbol. From time to time someone will ask me how many years apart my twin and I are, and although age does not matter, I will tell the person there are twelve and a half years between us in age. I am then reminded that the address of the church where I was baptized is 1212, yet another synchronicity which I was remembering recently.

All in all, I want to remind all twin flames — either newer ones who are newly awakened or other twin flames that have been on this path a long time — not to give up when you want to throw in the towel, as this can be a heart-wrenching journey at times. As I mentioned earlier, this journey is all about finding your true, authentic self and not needing anything outside of yourself. The journey is about shining your light where you have never been able to shine your light and showing up for yourself regardless of what others may say or think. I want to remind everyone that we all have a journey which we are truly living no matter if you are awakened or not. We all came here to be able to experience joy and love and to be proud of our accomplishments, and we do not need anyone's approval to accomplish these achievements or milestones.

To further highlight the many synchronicities in my life, the other day I received from my aunt a genealogy report from my paternal grandfather's side of the family. On the top of the first sheet was a baptismal certificate from St. Peter's Church in Brooklyn, New York, and my twin is currently an organ player in St. Peter's Church in South Boston. For twenty-three years, I also worked in South Boston at a trolley tour company. My grandmother was orphaned at the age of six and she was raised by her aunt. He has hosted orphaned children at Christmastime over the last few years. These many moments of synchronicities and parallel lives further indicate our unique twin soul connection to one another.

CHAPTER 6

Dreams

This chapter is about dreams. I dreamt of my twin flame so long ago. Over the last twenty to thirty years, I have always felt my twin around me. As I mentioned in previous chapters, twin flames share the same soul essence in two different bodies as well as the same energetic blueprint. When I was younger, I would pray that I would meet a man similar to my dad. On my birthday when I would blow out the candles, I would make a wish that I would meet someone like my dad whom I always looked up to. It makes sense now to me as my twin and I love to celebrate birthdays and celebrations as I mentioned in Chapter 5 that twins share many parallel lives and synchronicities. The man I dreamt about so long ago was the man I met in the fall of 2015 as my son's preschool teacher. The moment my son and I walked into his classroom, I felt at home within a few seconds. I mentioned in previous chapters that twin flames usually will meet one another when one or both are in committed relationships. The divine or God will orchestrate the right time for twin flames to meet here on Earth to begin the healing process of breaking down belief systems that are no longer in our highest and best interest for our growth. It is possible that twin flames can come together in the physical as long as they have healed all aspects of themselves and have detached from trying to control the outcome of how they will come together. The physical union is up to God and the divine.

The song that came to me while writing this chapter was Billy Joel's song, "River of Dreams." First, the song is about streams of consciousness and remembering why you came here and who you are meant to be, rather than dwelling in the old belief systems that put you into a box that will not let you, or make you feel that you cannot, freely express your true nature. "River of Dreams" reminds me, as well, that when you go searching for your authentic truth, you will find it as long as you let go of resistance and let the flow guide you to change and grow like a river, which is always flowing. We need to learn to flow as well. As a society we have this old belief system from ancestral patterns that we must learn to oblige and conform with when in reality we are here for a different reason entirely, to bring our gifts to reality. For instance, my twin plays the organ at masses, and he brings the gift of music to the world rather than allowing his gift to lie dormant and ignoring those gifts that have been bestowed on him since birth. So, too, must we all bring our gifts to the world.

When you dream about the person you always wanted to be with, the twin flame journey will completely remind you of this especially as a lot of twin flames have shared a past life together and have met again in this life on Earth to resolve what we as twin flames came here to accomplish. We are here to break down the stereotypical programming that has been placed on us. A year after my son had my twin as a preschool teacher in January of 2017, I was taking a walk in nature. When you are on a spiritual journey of any kind, it is best to connect with nature as well as to go within. When I was connecting to nature in January of 2017, I had a conversation with God and asked him to please show me a sign as I had all these feelings for my twin flame even after a year of my son no longer being in his class. I could not shake my feelings for him, so I asked that God please show me a sign to assure me that I was not crazy. The gift I received in nature was a red string of fate. I explained a bit of what a red string of fate means in Chapter 5, but I will elaborate more about what a red string of fate is as it is a gift I was given in nature at this time. A few days before I was given the red string of fate in nature by God, I had a dream as I had asked if I was on the right path with Charley and what it was that I needed to learn on this twin flame journey. I discovered that the purpose was to learn to have patience and wisdom.

I had had a dream of patience and wisdom in January of 2017 before God showed me the red string of fate. A red string of fate is a red thread that can be stretched, tangled up, and shrunken but never be broken, just as the bond of twin flames can never be broken no matter the time, distance, or circumstance. It doesn't matter where each twin is on the path to self-acceptance and love. A red string of fate connects you both at the heart and eye level. As I have been on the twin flame journey for some time, I have learned that twin flames are connected at both the heart and the eye level as the eyes are the windows to the soul. I want to reiterate to newer twin flames on the twin flame journey path that no matter the circumstance of where each of us is on our path, the bond between twin flames can never be broken no matter how hard people try to break this connection as it is all divinely orchestrated by God.

As I mentioned, I found the red string of fate in January of 2017 and in February of 2017 my twin gave me a "hug me" M&M with a string tied around three times which was when I realized how much we had a unique connection. As I have mentioned, twin flames experience sporadic communication, which can cause doubt from time to time, but the sporadic communication is meant to put you into a physical separation, so you can grow and evolve individually and become the best version of yourself. When twin flames have grown individually in this way they can merge together as one in divine timing. The separation is also something to help you get clear about your mission as well as to balance your feminine and masculine energies. It also serves to help you accept all aspects of yourself without needing validation from the external as this journey is all about connecting within and being comfortable being alone with yourself. Even though we have a strong connection to our twin flames, we still need not to push our twins, and we learn that each of us has our individualized paths that eventually will intertwine. We can learn to be in complete peace with ourselves and not look for external validation from anyone or anything outside of ourselves. This path is also about trust in ourselves, God, our twins, and knowing that God is in charge of when divine timing happens for everything. Again, we as a society have learned to try to have so much control of ourselves and others that we do not know the art of letting go and letting God lead and guide us through life.

Now I am going to talk about patience and wisdom. *Patience,* I thought, *oh okay, yes, I have lots of patience.* I soon realized that when

I had met my twin flame eight years ago, it was an example of how patience will be tested from time to time on this journey, but it is only to keep your authentic truth and not waiver and compromise yourself just to satisfy others. It is essential that you learn to do what you feel your intuition is guiding you to do. I know from my experience on this journey that twins will go into the expanding and contracting stage, when one twin may be ahead of another at times only to eventually merge. This process cannot be rushed. This is when patience, for sure, is what is required for yourself, God, your twin, and loved ones around you.

Wisdom I thought I knew for sure at the time of my dream back in January of 2017. Wisdom has helped me, as well, in the last eight years as we get to learn about ourselves and about what is in alignment for our true purpose here on Earth. It has taught me to learn along this journey and make the most of every day. You must remember to always be grateful in times of purging old belief systems that no longer are in alignment for your best self and to still stand strong despite things that you may need to let go of to become the best version of you. Wisdom has taught me that we are living a human soul experience as well as having soul awakening, and we are realizing how to adjust to both frequencies along the way, especially if you and your twins are empaths. We need to know how to teach and learn from the world at large, how to protect ourselves energetically, as well as how to become the beacon of light. People learn to ascend on the spiritual journey whether it be a twin flame path or a spiritual journey. We need to be able to assist our twin and others who will eventually be awakened in any capacity because as the title reiterates of this book *Twin Flames and How They Change Your World,* the twin flame experience literally does change and challenge your old way of thinking.

Speaking of dreams. . . let me say that it was through a dream that I got the title of my book in March of 2017. I saw a complete vision of the title of this book and over the last seven years, yes, I have had doubts about how and what I need to write as I am living both a human and soul experience as we all are. My advice to you is to get clear and because we are living a human experience as well as one on a soul level, we must take time, as I mentioned earlier in this chapter, to be able to go within and trust our intuition as we are all born with intuition. We can access our intuition any time we choose. I knew from the time I had a dream about the title of this book that I also needed to teach from this book, to have patience and wisdom along the way, and to learn to trust my dreams and, most importantly, my intuition. I learned in a Mediumship class, which I took a few years into this journey with the instructor Debbie McBride, that people should always have a dream journal by their bedside as a way to record their dreams as a dream may not be playing out at the exact moment you dream it. A dream can play out months or years down the road. I feel this is part of the wisdom along this journey which I needed to learn, among other things as well.

Earlier in this chapter I mentioned talking about Billy Joel's song, "River of Dreams" as there is a part of the song that speaks about the shadow of death. This verse reminds me of when you meet your twin flame, and after the bliss of finally meeting, you go into the stage called the dark knight of the soul in order to find the pieces of yourself that you have lost throughout your life. During this stage of the journey, we learn to acknowledge the dark shadows and suppressed feelings, emotions, and abilities within us and to work through a process of healing them. You eventually will come out of the dark knight of the soul only to get more clarity on this path or any path you are embarking on. Also, during the twin flame journey you learn a little at a time about how to let go of your ego as there are many stages on the twin flame journey. One stage is an ego death which feels like a dark knight of the soul coming to help you to remember the reason why you came here to Earth. You are reminded to not continue being subservient to others but rather to begin to place your needs first and start knowing how to balance your needs with the world at large. This, too, has been a lesson in wisdom along this journey, the wisdom to know how to balance your energies so you learn to set clear and concise boundaries, especially when you are following your dreams and intuition. As the saying goes, "Rome was not built in a day," we must surpass the lessons to climb the mountain to our destiny while always and consistently surrendering to it and continuing to live our lives each day as tomorrow is never promised.

As I mentioned earlier in this chapter, when you meet your twin flame, you feel you have come home at last and then, like in the fairy tale romances, you begin to wonder if this is real or made up in your mind, especially when you have been dreaming of someone for so long. You finally meet and, as a result, you start to take an inventory of your life and decide either to follow your heart and intuition or stay stuck and stagnant and not uncover the best version of yourself.

I will now write about the patience part of my dream. When I had the patience part of my dream come through, I was sure I had patience. My definition of patience was not the same as God. I am writing this for all of you, especially if you are new to the twin flame journey as your patience will be continually tested. I mentioned that all twin flames can go back and forth when one twin is ahead of the other. I am being reminded that this is not a race as we are living a soul connection as well as a human experience. We need to have lots of patience for ourselves, first and foremost, as we need to know how we can serve God in some capacity, and if we are able to have patience with ourselves, our twins and the rest of the world, then we can be of service. A few years back when I had the dream of patience and wisdom, I was 100 percent sure I had the qualities of patience and wisdom. Wisdom I thought for sure I had as well, as you know there is always learning on this path, or any path you embark upon. As I mentioned this is a soul connection, there is so much learning and growth that goes hand in hand when it comes to wisdom.

My twin Charles has shown me a lot of wisdom along the way. He showed me that it is okay to follow our passion and maintain the unique soul connection we have. One other person that stands out as having lots of wisdom was my dad. My dad was full of wisdom, and he was a true visionary. He would always take Sundays to plan out his week. He had to plan out each week for family, business, and what was most important in his life while quietly maintaining composure to get it all done and keep his faith in God. What the dream of wisdom means to me now, after meeting my twin Charles, is not to lose sight of what you want, as well as to spend quiet time to plan out what you want to see accomplished in this lifetime.

Now I know why God gifted me as I am reminded about the red string of fate I received in nature that shows how strong the connection is between twin flames. That first bond is so strong that it can never be broken no matter how many people may disapprove of the bond. It is orchestrated by God, and it is a soul connection as well. As we are also living a human experience, at times our human life can stall the process because we have societal demands that we must maintain like family, finances, and other obligations, but we continue to practice alignment to our spiritual connection.

As I mentioned, this journey cannot be rushed as we humans are so overprogrammed to want what we want when we want it instead of allowing the natural state of flow to occur. Instead of learning how to be in the moment of now and observing, we often react to everything from our ego. A song that recently came through my dream time was "Imagine," by John Lennon. I feel this song is significant as we are here to live in peace and follow our hearts and dreams, and we all can if we just allow ourselves to dream since anything is possible. The song also states that if we all followed our dreams, then the world would be as one. We are learning to live in a state of oneness, and we are not separate from one another. God created us as equals. The part of the song in "Imagine" where it says people shall live for today rings so true, especially on this twin flame journey path or any spiritual path. The more we can allow ourselves to go into heart space, the more we can follow our dreams and be at peace with ourselves and the rest of the world. It is hard for people to realize that they can have the dreams that they set out to have within reason. They should know and trust in God that they can have the dreams that they are working towards as long as they listen to and trust in God. You must let go of how to control and let it be and let God work on the details as long as you seek the change in you for yourself and not for anyone else. Another song that has come in my dreamtime is by Paul McCartney, "Let It Be." This song talks about wisdom, which ties into the dream I had a few years ago on wisdom. As humans, we tend to want control as we have learned this in societal programming instead of just allowing and letting God guide us with all the answers. The more we allow God into our lives, the more answers we will receive.

As I am writing this chapter, I am reminded of a spiritual experience with trust and wisdom. My friend Michael Lynch, who passed away in December of 2018, comes to mind. I was certified in kundalini reiki and helped him while he was transitioning from this life to the afterlife by sending him distance reiki energy. I am reminded when he knew that he was not going to get better, he had the choice of either fighting with all his might or just leaving it up to God to help in the transition as long as he made peace and resolved the worldly issues before he left the Earthly plane. This journey also reminds me that we must let go of resistance and let God lead us and listen to our heart and soul for the wisdom from within us.

One other thing that I want to reiterate as well is about when we meet our twin flames. Yes, we want to have both the physical and spiritual connection and that is possible as long as you leave enough room for God to work out the details and not just sit around and wait for your twin as this is a spiritual connection. You need to leave room for God's work and not just stay stuck and stagnant which can happen from time to time on this journey. You must not let the stuck energy consume you, but instead, you should work through it and use it to find and become the best version of you. I want to reiterate this, especially to all twin flames who have been on this journey for a long time as well as to newer twin flames. I know coming out from the bliss after you meet your twin flame and going into the dark knight of the soul is not an easy process, but it is meant for you to see the dark shadow elements that you have ignored and suppressed. To come out of the dark knight of the soul will help you get more clarity as well as help you find ways to choose peace and love and create a life you want from within. One other thing I was reminded of in the patience part of my dream was to have tons of patience with self as we are learning new ways to program our minds to better ourselves each and every day, and we will live our lives in peace the more we listen to God and remain still. I was also reminded in another dream I had at the beginning of this journey, and it was that through the Disney movies, where Prince Charming meets his princess, that we all are able to have this as long as we can believe in ourselves and love ourselves first and foremost. God wants what we want as long as we can trust and learn to go within and love ourselves first and learn to love all aspects of ourselves unconditionally. We are meant to have the love that we came here to experience. These movies were made to show us that love is real and that everyone has the opportunity for love in his or her life as long as he or she believes in him or herself and in God.

Twin flames must learn to not be too attached or controlling of one another as we are learning to trust and believe in ourselves and God. I will give you an example of my friends Paula and David, who remind me of being twin flames, as they are married and very much there for one another. But they also allow each other to grow in their relationship, so they continue to see the beauty within themselves and create and aspire to be the best versions of themselves without compromising and continuing to maintain their own power within the relationship. This came to me in a dream as well because a lot of twin flames are learning to set better boundaries for themselves, and they are taking back their power where they, somewhere along the way, gave their power away. Every so often I have asked God what else it is that I need to learn on this journey. I learn that I need to take back my power and stay in my authentic truth while not compromising myself. That is why I see my friends Paula and David as having strong boundaries and not compromising themselves but loving from within while understanding one another. The reason why I am writing this in my dream section of this chapter is to show you that although we have such a strong connection with our twins, we must not forget that this journey is about learning how to love and accept all aspects of ourselves and to believe in ourselves. It is important to find ways in which you can be your true authentic self and not attach to the stories of being unworthy of love. We are all here to learn lessons to help us grow and evolve and let go of the old and love always.

In another dream I recently had about wisdom was based on a book that I am reading, *The Power of Now,* by Eckhart Tolle. One chapter which is similar to what I was reminded of in my dreams is that on this twin flame journey, or any journey, you must try to remain in observance mode. Observance mode means to stay in present thought. This is very useful as our minds always either take us to the past or future and we do not know how to stay in the present. This is also a part of the wisdom dream I had a few years back as well as one recently. The more we can learn to stay in the present moment, forgive our past, and observe the moment instead of going to the future where we build expectations, the better it will be. We have learned to build up expectations only to be disappointed which then leads to the need to forgive ourselves and others for the unrealistic expectations of the past.

I am including this important idea as it is a key element to learn on the twin flame journey because we all have expectations of what our twins should or shouldn't be doing instead of allowing and trusting that God will help you along this journey. Instead, we try to control everything every step of the way instead of surrendering and putting the focus back on ourselves and becoming one with God. We as a society are so used to controlling or being controlled that we do not know how to just be and stay present. Society has taught us through movies, TV, and family patterns that controlling and being controlled is okay, but it is not, since God is the one in control and he knows what is best for all of us. This is where we have lost trust in ourselves and others, and at times, we tend to look outside ourselves instead of going within and remaining in the present.

I feel this is part of the wisdom dream I had recently, as well as seven years ago. The reading that I heard at mass yesterday from the first letter of Paul to the Corinthians sums up the dream I had four and a half years ago about what it is that my twin Charles and I came here to learn. This reading summed it up perfectly. We read about how Jesus, or whomever you believe in, phrases it perfectly that he did not know too much and instead of being one that thought he knew everything, he came to us through learning, trusting, and listening to God. He knew he had weakness and fear, but he teaches us to trust in God and the path that you are on as we are all God's children and God has a divine plan for each and every one of us. However, we have all been trained to protect our ego lifetime after lifetime, especially if we are an empath as many twins are. At times, twin flames have not learned to trust themselves as they often give of themselves and have not learned to listen and trust their own intuition. The priest through his homily yesterday stated it perfectly that we are the salt of the Earth and light workers, who are people who spread love and light through God's work. He mentioned in his homily that we can be light workers even if we sometimes have doubts. We need trust in God as God is always within all of us. Sadly, we have learned at such a young age to look outside of ourselves instead of becoming still and going within. We must remember that we have all the answers within to know what is right for us and how to serve God and one another. We must work at becoming one instead of creating a world of being separate from one another as we all have gifts, as I stated earlier, that God has bestowed on each and every one of us. We must trust, learn, and have patience and wisdom along the way especially when we do not have an immediate answer. The answer will come as long as you have patience and can learn to still your mind and listen to your heart. All the answers within you come through the heart and soul.

This sums up the dream I had when my twin Charles awakened me, and I kept questioning if I was on the right path. Yes, indeed, I was on the right path and I have been learning how to trust in myself and God. The two readings at Church yesterday provided an "aha" moment to the dream I had before I found the red string of fate in nature and the dreams about patience and wisdom. Patience and wisdom are the most important to have on the twin flame journey or any journey you are on. As the gospel stated yesterday that we are all the salt of the Earth and the priest explains this perfectly. We can be the salt of the Earth or light workers even if we have insecurities. We must trust in God as God lives within us, just as the song from *The Lion King* tells us. Both the song and the priest mention that he lives within us and, no matter whom you believe in, we must trust in God and our inner guidance. Sometimes the answers don't come to us when we want them, and that is when patience comes in. Especially when you are awakened by your twin, you are never alone, as twins are always uniquely connected, but we must not give up on ourselves, God, our twin and the world around us as we have our paths we must walk to ultimately to merge as one.

It takes lots of patience and wisdom through the twin flame journey, or any journey you are on, as we have to learn patience and wisdom along the way, and it may take a few lessons to finally correct the patterns we are learning to let go of in order to serve God and have love for a better tomorrow. I basically want to remind you to trust in the process and let God guide you every step of the way even though this journey can have twists and turns and feel like a roller coaster ride. At times on the twin flame journey, one twin may be ahead of the other as the role reversal happens from time to time. We are still learning lessons on this path, as we are learning to connect our soul and human experience while living in a 3D reality. We need to learn to balance both 3D living as well as balance our spiritual connection. Twin flames must learn how to balance our 3D human reality and our 5D spiritual reality to come together in a balanced state on a 3D level. Finding the red string of fate in nature and listening to the homily solidified that the spiritual 5D and the human 3D level connection that Charley and I have with one another all comes down to patience and wisdom on a human level in divine timing. This is true not only for us but also for other twin flame unions. We need to balance these two realities on a human level to serve God and to create love. My experience of the red string and the priest's homily assured me that it takes time for your soul and human experience to merge on a human level. I realized I was on the right path with my twin Charles. The readings and homily yesterday solidified everything that I have been learning on this path back to love and acceptance for myself, God, and my twin flame.

CHAPTER 7

Empaths

This chapter is about twin flames being empathetic. All my life I have been an empathic person, since the moment I was in utero when my mom was pregnant with me. Even before I was born, I helped her get through the loss of two of her sisters. From this time on, I was always a healer, desiring to heal and take on the world and its pain and suffering. It is a great quality to be empathic, although at times it can hinder your relationship to self and to those around you whom you love. Being an empath can be difficult at times as you want to give to everyone in the world, and at the end of the day, you have nothing left to give to yourself, and you often feel depleted. A lot of twin flames are empathetic because, similar to my experience, they have chosen, since even before their birth, not only to meet in this life but also to heal the world at large in the capacity that they are drawn to.

When you meet your twin flame, you realize that up until this point, you have missed the opportunity to have this awesome relationship to self, as you are both mirrors of one another, as well as polar opposites. You can have that ultimate relationship with your twin flame although it takes many lifetimes as you both have to clear a lot of patterns of self-worth within each of you because you are both empaths. You learn to balance yourself out along the way and to check in with yourself on a daily basis to find out if it is your own energy or someone else's energy you are taking on. As empaths, we can feel everything around us. Even if we are walking by someone, we can feel their sadness. At the end of the day, I recommend for all empaths and twin flames to nurture themselves every day by taking a salt bath, having tea, and finding a quiet place to meditate to find their center. As I mentioned earlier, twin flames are a mirror of one another, so upon meeting your twin flame, you realize you have not been kind with yourself through lifetimes.

We, as empaths, have always taken on other people's emotions whether good, bad, or indifferent. It is a great quality to be empathetic although when taking on someone else's sadness or loneliness, you do not realize you are absorbing someone else's energy, as you can all of a sudden feel sad, depressed, or lonely. My advice to you is to do a clearing meditation to clear the energies you have absorbed each day. Empaths crave a lot of alone time even after they have become awakened, as the experience of being empathetic literally shakes up your world in every sense. The awakening feels like huge waves crashing over you and challenging you in every aspect of yourself. Twin flames are here to bring unconditional love back to themselves, first and foremost, as well as to create unconditional love with one another and the rest of the world at large. As twin flames, we are here to bring love and light to the world. Yesterday, for example, I was in a car dealership getting an oil change, and I was sitting in the waiting area and I asked God/ Universe what I and the rest of the world needed to know through this pandemic in 2020, and it was the fact that people are still divided in darkness and it is time to let the light in rather than to stay in darkness. During this time that we are in self-quarantine, as much as we can be, it is a time to turn inward and face the fears and not let the fear get the best of us. Instead, we must turn fear into something positive which can help us find out what we want out of life and what our purpose is.

The lights flickered and half the room was in dark and half was in light. It was a reminder of where we are at this time of our lives and how we can be still and not judge ourselves or one another, as I know we humans often judge. It is a part of the human condition. We must remember that God still loves us no matter what, and he loves us always. It is also the time to be still and know where your soul is guiding you at this time. We as twin flames decided at the time of birth to take on the role of empathy, and it is when we meet our twin flames here on

Earth that the healing must take place of breaking down patterns of belief systems.

I am guided to write about this now, as with the virus, we must take care of ourselves before we lend a helping hand. In addition, all the systems through this pandemic are shutting down only to show us later after the pandemic has quieted us down and shown us how to restructure our lives in new ways. We are now given an opportunity to be open to ways in which we can improve, instead of hinder, one another's abilities, talents, and anything that people came here to be. We can find the compassion within and strive for a better tomorrow. As twins we came here to live a life of love and light rather than always taking on the emotions of others. Through healing, once you have met your twin, you learn to clear and transmute all kinds of energies that we have either taken on over lifetimes or on a day-to-day basis. We are asked to let go of constraints that we as a society have learned to place on one another through healing ourselves and the family patterns we have agreed to take on. As an empath, we need to learn self-respect and self-worth because we are learning how to balance our feminine and masculine energy. If you are all too much in your feminine energy, then you tend to take on others' emotions, and it is important to take the time for yourself to nurture yourself. We are constantly breaking down patterns of belief systems, as there are a lot of times where we need to find the balance to rest and recharge our battery, so we can learn to break these old paradigms and learn how to come back into love for ourselves, our twins and the world. We are here to bring the love and light back to planet Earth.

Most of the twin flames that I have met along this journey have always been empathetic all of their lives. We tend to have a hard time with self-love, as we tend to other people's needs before our own. This is why it is so important when meeting your twin flame, or having had an awakening of any sort, that you practice self-love and also learn how to set clear and concise boundaries, learn not to be codependent, and learn how to detach without expectations. You must have trust and faith in God and unconditional love for yourself, first and foremost, before you can give of yourself to serve God in any capacity. As I mentioned in previous chapters as well, when twin flames come together, they are here together to build a beautiful mission to create more love and light on the Earth. Because we are empaths, lots of twin flames are drawn to careers serving humanity. The careers we are led to are in psychology and sociology, as well as customer service positions, because we love helping people. Twin flames usually have a child who is empathetic as well. I know my son Youssef is an empath as well as. He does better in smaller groups, as he can feel things deeper on an intuitive level. For example, when my twin flame was Youssef's teacher, and when he was out of school, my son felt his teacher's absence on a deeper level and was so sad that he was out of school for a day or two.

Further, many empaths always have tangent talks to themselves or with family members as they go from one conversation to another very quickly because they want to fix the world's issues all at once. People who are not empaths have a hard time keeping up with individuals who are empathetic since we continue wanting to serve humanity which can sometimes serve us in awesome ways as well as drain us. One other important thing through life for empaths is that they need to find a relaxing sport to help them calm their bodies. Yoga and dance or Zumba or even swimming and being around water are quite healing for empaths. I myself have always been drawn to water as I grew up swimming and spending time around water. As a child, people would often tell me that I would use too much water in daily activities, but the sounds of water running would be soothing to me. When I would do chores as a child, I would always be drawn towards anything to do with water.

Being an empath and meeting your twin flame can also be intense because both of you are empaths, and you both need to know how to calm and relax yourselves and find ways in which your inner being is cleared of so much clutter and noise in your head. I write this as empaths are constantly in their heads and not in their heart space and constantly questioning their every move. This is why it is so important to have a lot of down time away from the hustle and bustle of life. When we get stuck in our heads, sometimes it can lead to anxiety, and then we need to learn how to take deep, relaxing breaths. A lot of empaths tend to procrastinate as they know deep down in their heart and soul where they are being guided and what needs to be done. We always second-guess our intuition to satisfy someone else's needs, wants or desires instead of tuning in to our own intuition and desires. We have trouble trusting ourselves and others around us. This is why it is so important to unplug from society to draw back your power and relax into your heart space as your heart and soul will not lead you down the wrong path. We just need to trust the process and continue to listen to our intuition. I know ever since I was awakened by my twin flame Charley, I always second-guess everything although when I sit in quiet meditation without the noise in my head, then I know I am on the right path. As I have mentioned I heard I needed to write this book about thirty years ago, and I kept thinking I was hearing things. Then, about a year into my awakening, I finally got the title and vision of the book I am writing: *Twin Flames and How They Change Your World*. This title is appropriate as it truly does change everything you thought you knew to be true and completely makes you stop and take inventory of your life and which parts of yourself you have hidden away for so long.

Through the healing work, I have changed ingrained behavioral patterns, and I continue to break down these patterns that no longer serve me in my life. It is a constant struggle to change patterns of codependency and boundaries, especially for an empath who wants to take on the world and then does not take care of him or herself. This is why this is the perfect time when we are in lock-down mode just to sit and evaluate what we want to accomplish and how we hope to accomplish it. I know I am learning to take care of myself right now, which is a hard thing to do during this time of lock-down. I am teaching myself and showing other empathetic people to slow down and continue to follow their heart and soul and to still the mind as well as meditate. As empaths, we have a hard time to quiet our minds, which then leads to not trusting our intuition.

Personally, I have decided to make a change that I have needed to make during this time frame. It is to finish my book and through this book, there are important messages to share with the world at large. The message is to have a better understanding of what empaths are as well as to understand twin flames. As empaths we tend to chase after more than one thing at a time, something which then causes chaos in our heads since we want to fix the world. Empaths are in apologetic mode as they constantly feel guilty when they cannot attend to someone else's needs and they need to take care of themselves. That is why creating a space for meditation and using crystals will help them to find a balance. When they are around people, empaths are constantly being drained of their energy. Also creating a sacred space is a necessity for an empath to do, so they can unwind at the end of the day. A good balanced diet is a necessity for an empath as some people who have been empaths build up walls around themselves and they are afraid to trust others. They turn to comfort food to protect themselves as well. Being conscious about what you eat when you have become awakened will help you get through the ascension process a bit easier. Make sure that you limit your intake of sugar and eat lots of proteins and vegetables. Drinking plenty of water, getting plenty of rest and taking nature walks are helpful ways as well for empaths to raise their vibration and stay in a positive mindset.

Empaths have to constantly learn how to stay present and, in the moment, not let their minds take them in many directions all at once. As I stated above, empaths go on many tangents, so staying focused and present is a key to the healing process as well. As I am writing this chapter about being an empath, I want to encourage you to stop, listen and see the beauty in everything and to help you remain in your center with calmness and peace. Another important thing for an empath to do is to find a hobby or creativity. For example, singing, painting, writing, and dancing are some ways in which an empath can find his or her creativity. Empaths are free spirits and especially if you are born under the fire sign of Sagittarius or Aries. We are the adventurous types and have a hard time sitting still. I am writing this chapter as we as a society are going through a pandemic, and being a fire sign, I want to just get out and about and not sit and shelter in place. It is challenging but necessary to recalibrate and to take inventory through this time instead of constantly being in flight or fight mode. You can accomplish things that you came here to accomplish which, for me, is writing and finishing this book. For another empath, it could be music, painting, or drawing or just allowing the natural flow to come through. Empaths carry a trait of being both passive and aggressive as we learning how to balance these personal characteristics. Being passive, you do not want to create drama in your life, although it can be hinder an empath as it can hurt the relationship to self and others if you allow other people to constantly walk all over you and are not able to set loving boundaries for yourself and others around you. When empaths do what we they do best by being passive, they know deep down in their heart and soul that they do not want to hurt anyone and they wish to avoid as much conflict just to keep the peace. However, being too passive can then lead to aggressive behaviors and anger. Other empaths, like myself, are constantly having to find the balance between being passive and aggressive. Too much passivity can lead to anger and aggression, which are the last things that an empath wants to feel as we are here to serve God and balance this out through our healing. If you are too passive, you tend to want to hide away, but then when you become awakened, as I did, you are forced to stop hiding and step out of your comfort zone in order to find balance. I know that I am always balancing between passive and aggressive thoughts and behaviors as I also am constantly battling not to be too much in my ego. We empaths want to share with the world our gifts and talents without being too much in ego.

As I am writing this chapter, I am listening to my friend Chad LaMarsh sing a song, "Say What You Need to Say." The original artist is John Mayer and this song reminds me and other empaths as well to speak up and tell people how we feel as it is important to speak up and not stay hidden for the rest of our lives. God gave us all a voice to use in a positive way whether that is through music, writing, or art. God wants us to be able to grow and evolve and not stay stuck all our lives. That is why it is important to be able to open up as an empath and learn how to balance being passive or aggressive through our healing as we become awakened.

Unfortunately, empaths sometimes tend to turn to alcohol or food to comfort their emotions, so as the saying goes: *It is better to be seen and not heard.* As empaths we internalize a lot just as I stated earlier to avoid conflict which is not good at all. Once on the healing path, we are always learning to balance knowing the right time to speak up and not cause waves. We empaths learn to comfort ourselves with food and alcohol. I know about this challenge. When I heard I needed to write this book, first off, I thought I was hearing things. It was already back thirty years ago as I met my soulmate Bob Cirame, whom I ran from at the time. Years later I cried and cried, and back then, because I was an empath, I would use food, alcohol, or diet pills to suppress my feelings. Rather than cope with my feelings in a healthy way, I ran away from my feelings.

Once I met Charley, I really made the effort not to suppress my emotions and I turned to writing. I chose to heal all aspects of myself and not keep up these past patterns as I am worthy of love for self and worthy of having a kind and loving relationship with self and another. When I was first awakened by Charley back in 2015-2016 and by the summer of 2016, I chose to heal this negative and destructive pattern. Instead of running from how I felt. instead of turning to alcohol, food, or diet pills to cope with my feelings, I began to choose a healthy path of self-awareness and strength. I realized that as an empath, I had the tendency to avoid conflict at any cost and to turn to these comfort foods or alcohol. Back thirty years ago, I was confused about my life path. I mistakenly thought I could take on the world and take on others' issues, which led me down a destructive path of codependency. Many empaths have known codependent relationships or addicting relationships to self and others, and they too often attract relationships that are not fulfilling to their soul growth. Throughout the awakening experience that empaths go through, it is best to heal your relationship with self before you can give of yourself and you must fill your cup of love for yourself. We are deserving and worthy of love, but we must take the time to be and to know ourselves and really go within to heal which, as an empath and a fire sign, I am and you are constantly in flight or fight mode. It is hard to sit with our feelings, but this can be achieved through self-awareness and effort. The more you can sit with your feelings and not run from them and, instead, heal all aspects of yourself for the better version of you, the better you will feel. Deep breathing meditation is definitely a necessity for an empath since we can become drained very easily as we are drawn to all types of energies. At some point during each day, it is best to find a way to meditate and practice deep breathing meditations to help us get through the day - one moment, one minute, and one day at a time. We empaths are too concerned with the world outside of ourselves and need to constantly pull back our energy, so we can better serve God and serve in a way that we do not feel depleted. That is why meditation, deep breathing and carrying crystals will help you to take back your energy and to keep centered. Throughout life, empaths tend to overwork and not take time to play or enjoy time away from responsibility. I know, myself, when I am being too serious, so I am always reminded to take time to play, to stop and smell the roses as the saying goes.

Another important thought occurs to me during this time of a health pandemic. As empaths, we are constantly being reminded to shift our energy so as not to stay stagnant. As empaths feel so much of the energy and the feelings of others around us, during this time of a global pandemic, we must stay strong in our belief as an empath and move towards our goals and aspirations which we came here to fulfill. We are here to serve through God, to keep allowing and trusting in God and to trust in the goals and the aspirations that we have been brought here to accomplish. We are here to serve and not to feel guilty or ashamed. We must remember not to shift or alter our thinking just to please others as we have done all our lives. I know for all my life it is has been difficult as I have been wanting to fix the world at large as an empath, but I have had to constantly work on the necessary things that are important for my growth and evolution rather than focusing on everything outside of me. This is my challenge as an empath, especially now. We empaths are so used to shifting our focus to accommodate others and as we shift into this reality, this new paradigm, it is difficult but it can be achieved! You must guard against going in too many directions and stay strong and focused on what messages come through to you and how you can serve God through the messages. You must stay clear and determined to accomplish the work you came here to do and really conscientiously pull back your energy when you feel you are extending your energy in the wrong places.

For me and other empaths on the twin flame journey, it is necessity to take a step back, breathe and remain centered and focused on your life purpose and continue to nurture yourself along the way as we tend to want to look outside of ourselves instead of turning inwards. I know throughout life and even as a small child, I have always been in fight or flight mode as I have often felt I needed to tend to something or someone outside of myself which I have now come to understand and know not to be true. Of course, many of us are learning to work on unraveling the layers one day at a time but it does not happen overnight. It can and will be achieved as I, and other empaths like me, learn how to nurture all aspects of ourselves without feeling lots of guilt. Guilt is one trait we empaths have taken on lifetime after lifetime only to find out we have depleted our energies by giving of ourselves too freely.

As a small child, I learned to do that, especially as I mentioned above, in utero with my mom as I was helping her through grief as she lost both of her sisters within a year from one another. I also know after my near-death experience at age eight, I have always pushed myself beyond my limits, so much so that I did not stop and nurture myself because I wanted to take on the world at large between both of these experiences – helping my mom with her grieving and nearly passing away at such a young age. My thoughts and behavior actually created more destructive than healthy patterns. As an empath I, myself, and other empaths who are twin flames, constantly put themselves last and have to find new ways to balance and take care of themselves first. Finding new ways to balance these energies is a struggle, but it can be achieved through a more conscious and consistent effort in the healing process.

Empaths value their alone time especially whether in a committed relationship with their twin flame or soulmate or anyone else, as they need their space to decompress lots of energies they pick up throughout the day. Sometimes we do not know where it comes from. This is why journaling and meditation are the key to healing on our spiritual journey. Empaths really need to find that alone time to center themselves. This was even emphasized in a recent video. My soul sisters Donna and Naglaa were talking about how we empaths want to take on the world, yet sometimes we need to shut down and know how we can balance what we can take on and what is not ours. We just want to be able to heal the world and, at the same time, filter our emotions properly. It is like reiki, when you are sending someone healing but making sure not to take on emotions of another individual as it is will become part of your energy field. That is why we first need to have our alone time and find ways to ground our energies.

My dad was for sure an empath and through his life here on Earth, he taught me and he still shows me signs about how to balance being an empath and how I can heal myself and the world. He guides me to continue to find the joy along the way and not to get caught up in all the energies and to learn to focus without being so distracted. For empaths diet is important to follow a plant-based and an organic type diet and to avoid too much food that has a lot of sugar, as empaths tend to gravitate to all types of food. So, it is vital to find conscious ways to eat healthy foods, as that will help our mood elevate instead of gravitating towards sugar. I am writing this as personally, and as an empath, I was always drawn to food as a way to cope and build walls, and I had a hard time trusting others. Every time I took on another person's issue, I thought it was my own issue, and through the healing in reiki, I am learning that is not my job to absorb others' energies and problems. When you are learning how to do reiki, you learn that you have to be a clear channel and consciously not absorb others' energy as we, as empaths, can quickly do so.

Empaths need to stay present instead of becoming consumed by the chaos in our heads, and we learn as we go, that we are here to heal the world and not to take on the world all by ourselves. One other important healing for an empath is to be able to forgive yourself, as the world we live in is a imperfect perfect world. As empaths, we are constantly feeling we have to be perfect when that is just not true or even possible. This is why forgiving oneself and those around you will help you in your healing process to better understand yourself and the world, so you can better serve God and others in the world around you. A song that came to me as I have been writing this chapter about empaths is Alanis Morissette's, "You Learn." This resonates for myself and others who are empaths that we must slow down and learn to love all aspects of ourselves, so we know how to balance our lives to help others and ourselves. Especially, if we need to cry, we should allow ourselves to cry as we cannot keep taking on the emotions of someone else, something empaths do best and must guard against. The song goes on to mention that we should avoid taking on too much and we should focus on our heart's desires. These resonate as we empaths often find ourselves knee deep in things, and we do not know how to slow down or to catch a breath. We can let the chaos subside so that we can follow our hearts and not get caught in fixing others, as we all came here to learn our own lessons. It is through lessons and healing that empaths learn to navigate their way along the spiritual journey to create a better life.

CHAPTER 8

Incarnate

When meeting your twin flame, there is usually an age gap. The difference in age can vary from ten to forty years. As I mentioned, my twin and I have a twelve-and-a-half-year age difference. Usually when twin flames have an age difference and plan to incarnate on Earth together, they live parallel lives, which I mentioned in another chapter. When I say that we live parallel lives, I mean that we twin flames go through the same experiences at separate times in our lives. We may even have the same type of career, or we may major in the same type of study. I write about the age difference as this is one of the differences some twin flames have to learn to accept the age gap, as this is one of the incarnations that we go through and this is one of the familial templates that we learn to break from our societal programming. Twin flames go through many incarnations to learn to break ancestral patterns that have been instilled in them from generation to generation. Through our incarnations we learn to love ourselves, our twin flames, and others around us and not to place conditions on anyone. Worthiness and self-acceptance are huge incarnations and major lessons we learn because, as I mentioned in my chapter on being empathetic, we tend to others' needs before we tend to our own needs, which at times can be a constant struggle. At the same time, we learn to put ourselves first, so we do not feel depleted by someone else's demands and needs.

As I am writing this chapter, I am being reminded of when I traveled to my twin flame's hometown of Hyattsville, Maryland, and I asked God if being there in order to ground energy for our union was the right spot when, literally, I looked up and an infinity symbol appeared in the sky just as I looked up and asked the question. I feel the infinity symbol correlates to incarnation, as we twin flames and our relationship with one another are always infinite; our connection with our twin flame is always infinite despite the length of time we spend with one another in the physical union together. Twin flames are always supporting one another through our incarnations, through our heart and soul, and the more we can open our heart and soul, the more we can open up our hearts to the pure heart and soul connection of our twin flame counterparts.

As I am writing this chapter, I am listening to my friend Chad LaMarsh sing "Iris," which was originally sung by the Goo Goo Dolls. The first verse of the song reminds me of the twin flame journey when you meet your twin flame and your life is meant to be broken in order to discover who you are. At first, it does not feel like that, as it feels all bliss when you meet your twin and part of the journey through the incarnations is to allow for your life to be broken to allow for transformations to begin in an individual and then in a collective experience. The first part of the song "Iris" mentions when everything is made to be broken, and it correlates well with this journey to finally be able, as individuals, to stop running from what we came here on Earth to accomplish. This is why when you have met your twin, it takes many lifetimes to believe in your dreams and feel worthy as you have to constantly let go of societal programming and ancestral patterns to believe in who you are and how you came here to accomplish your life's purpose on this new Earth. Twin Flames come into one another's lives to learn lessons, which is all part of the incarnating process, and to recognize our talents and gifts that have lay dormant for so long until we awaken each other in the activating process.

Just recently I came upon a quote which I feel is appropriate to this chapter of the incarnating process. The quote is as follows: 1 Corinthians 12:4-5 NABRE "There are different kinds of spiritual gifts, but the same spirit; there are different forms of service, but the same Lord." I feel this quote to be appropriate as when twin flames awaken one another throughout the years, our gifts become amplified as we are being led to be in service to do God's work and for humanity. Another song that my friend Chad sings that I also feel is appropriate to this twin flame journey is called, "Say Goodbye," as it is a reminder on this twin flame journey that you can only ignore the journey for so long, as I, like others, have done from time to time. Instead of always being in your head space, this journey is to remain in your heart and soul, as this as another lesson in incarnating, as we have a tendency because of societal programs to be more in logic and head space rather than in our heart space. There is a part of the song, "Say Goodbye," which reminds us that your twin or the other person is not to blame as you will constantly hear your twin's name or see the synchronicity no matter what only to remain in your heart and soul space. Part of the song says that you cannot fight this connection nail and tooth, which is so similar to the twin journey. You can only battle your head and heart for so long until you keep surrendering and not let your head overtake your heart and soul. Basically, you are the one to blame and no one else is, whether it be a twin flame or someone else, as you are the one to choose love and heart and soul space instead of headspace. It takes time to heal and that is why we cannot rush the process of healing, as twins through incarnating learn to heal and not always be in logic and head space and remain in heart and soul space as the soul is the compass to our life purpose and destiny.

When we learn to listen to our heart, beautiful transformations can begin if we allow ourselves to remain in our heart and soul. I feel "Say Goodbye" correlates with the twin flame journey as the more we deny our own happiness, the longer it takes to continue learning lessons in our incarnations over and over instead of being still and just letting God and our angels guide us. We must continue to listen to the whispers of our heart and soul. Another song that came through to me this week, as well, was a song from the group U2, "Cradle to the Grave," which I feel is a powerful message. As the song says, we are all born with a blueprint of our destiny and we have to decide if we are going to fulfill our promise here on Earth. As mentioned in another chapter, I wrote that I heard I needed to write a book thirty years ago. When you hear things, at first you think you are not hearing correctly until you are awakened by your twin flame. A year into my awakening, I saw the title of this book in my vision and, just recently, I know now that my guides are definitely encouraging me to finish my story.

As I was driving down Route 9 in Wellesley, Massachusetts thirty years ago, I heard that I needed to write a book although at the time did not hear the whisper until my twin Charley awakened me, and then recently, I was driving on the same road and a white hawk nearly missed my car. The meaning behind it was to continue to focus on you and your dreams and not to to let outside distractions get in your way. We as a society can get so easily distracted and that I feel is another lesson in incarnating, as we are programmed to worry about other things outside our environment rather than focusing on our own destiny. This is definitely a pattern that we need to break. I know in my experience, we get so wrapped up with our daily lives that we almost need to make a schedule, so we can still get things accomplished in small increments rather than huge increments. We as a society are so used to being pulled in so many directions and instead of stopping and breathing. Especially if you are an empath like I am, we put others' needs before our own. At the end of the day, you feel like you have not accomplished your "to do" list as my mom would say.

Getting back to the song by U2, "Cradle to the Grave," I feel it relates well, as it is a reminder for me to finish my book, which still needs to be told. I also feel writing this chapter on incarnation is especially important at this time when our world is being challenged. We are in observation mode, whether we want to change our reality or live the same way and not evolve. With the pandemic and the protests, we learn how we can grow and decide if we want to evolve or keep on incarnating in the same way by repeating lessons from ancestral patterns and societal programming that we have grown accustomed to. We all have a choice to grow and evolve if we just trust how God is guiding us, as I mentioned that our soul is the compass to our destiny. Through the twin flame journey on a soul level between all our incarnations with our twin flame, we help one another move past our greatest fears. We are each other's best teachers and muses as we teach one another not to shy away or hide away from our gifts and talents. Through our incarnations as we grow on this journey, we will feel a huge shift as the connection is more about coming into oneness and union with God and being able to love ourselves unconditionally, love our twin unconditionally and come into harmony with God. our twin and everyone around us as we are the light of the Earth. We are always united with God and are always one within. Because as humans living on a soul level, we are learning how we let people control us and when it comes down to it, we do not own anyone or anything, as we are shifting into a new way to be set free of programming. Generation after generation, we, as humans, have learned not to trust our intuition, which then led to us making or not making decisions for ourselves instead of going with our instinct on the first try. Twin flames have a soul plan to incarnate to learn to teach through writing, as I do, or through music, as my twin plays the organ at church, or through any creative endeavor that is meant for their calling to serve God.

As I am writing this chapter, I am being reminded of the movie *Blinded by the Light* and in the movie there is a song by Bruce Springsteen called "Thunder Road." This song references or speaks about the promised land and how we have all come here to speak our truth and that we need to trust and not hide away our fears in order to be able to open up and express our emotions in all ways and not be afraid of another person or other people, as everyone's views are different. We love one another unconditionally no matter the circumstance, and we learn to love ourselves and stand up for what we believe even if someone is not on the same page. I am being reminded in the movie of *Blinded by the Light* that the young boy in the film, Javad, had views different than his father. His father and he had very different views on culture. Throughout the movie, the son questioned if he would ever make his father understand his view or if he would succumb to his father's view on culture or religion. In fact, the young man stood in his power as he knew that he was here to write and speak his truth instead of hide away although his culture did not believe in speaking up. The ways of his family and culture taught people just to take orders and continue to repeat the lesson of incarnations by just doing as your told and not being seen. He ended up proving that you can love unconditionally and still have different viewpoints and that we must allow others be able to be free to express their feelings and opinions instead of suppressing what they are passionate about. In the movie *Blinded by the Light* the young boy learned he had to break the chains of ancestral patterns to teach his family that he was different, as he would always love his family unconditionally and at the same time, he needed to break down the barriers of his culture to show that everyone has a right to speak his or her mind. The story shows us that we should not conform or bend for someone else, but rather we should remain true to our center, to our core beliefs. I feel this a valuable lesson, as humanity needs to remain centered and people can speak their minds without the fear of being judged because, at the end of the day, God does not judge. He does not want anger of any sort, and he wants all to live in peace and harmony without succumbing to someone else's wishes or desires. As a nation we have learned this through ancestral patterns and somewhere along the line, the patterns need to be broken as we have to learn to accept ourselves for who we are and, in turn, we will accept our twin and the rest of humanity as one, as we are all God's children who speak many tongues. The movie *Blinded by the Light* relates to why we as individuals incarnate on Earth. We are here to teach valuable lessons to humanity, to show that there is more than one answer to a situation and to share the idea that we all have the right to voice our opinions without fear as God gave us voice to be our true authentic selves. The music of Bruce Springsteen inspires a Muslim teen to find his voice and follow his dreams. I am writing about this in the incarnate section of this book as I feel this relates to why we incarnate to find our own way and not to let our heads get in the way of our hearts. I feel that is why we all incarnate here on Earth to learn this lesson until we stop the cycle of searching outside of ourselves and continue listening to our intuition which helps us grow and evolve.

As I am writing this chapter, my son is on a Zoom call with his teacher, Ms. Cox, and he is learning how we all have differences and we need to learn to accept people for who they and to treat all people fairly. She gave an example of all people including twins, and I feel that relates to biological twins as well as twin flames and all humanity. We accept the person for who he or she is on all levels although the more work we do within and heal, the more we treat people with respect. It begins within. We know that we can accept people for who they are although we also need to stop judging ourselves harshly. I am learning along the way that treating ourselves and others with kindness starts within and one day, one moment at a time, we continue to trust ourselves and love and accept where we are on our journey. This, in turn, helps us accept our twin flame counterparts and everyone else, as we continue to raise our consciousness and continue to learn the lessons here. In one part of *Blinded by the Light,* the teacher in the movie asks the students why we are here. One of the students replies, "To make a difference, change the world and tell the world what it needs to hear." I know when we can stop the cycle and begin to step into our own, then we can begin to tell the world our story. What makes all of us unique is that we learn to shine our light to where it is needed in the world. People have the right to speak their truth and hold space for where people are at in life as we can only change within ourselves.

The more we tend to look outside ourselves and place too many judgments on self, the more we have to learn this through our incarnations that we have no right to judge ourselves. God is the one who always helps us love ourselves and others unconditionally without placing conditions on people. What comes to my mind is the lesson my son is learning about standing up for what we believe as it is our right and freedom to have our voices heard. Through my own experience and the experiences of other humans, we are learning through our incarnations to break down these conditions, which prevent us from being able to speak our truth and cause us to feel we have to continually run and hide just because someone does not want to hear the truth. We cannot make someone love us by placing demands on them. We just need to trust and keep on telling the truth and be able to constantly stand in our authentic truth without wavering. One song in my son's book in a reading lesson with his teacher is called "This Little Light of Mine," and it relates well to this chapter about incarnations. It reminds us to go towards the light, shine our light, and speak our truth. We must also remember that all people will not always agree with one another and we have to learn to accept that we may not always see eye to eye and that is okay.

One quote that comes to mind that my dad loved was, "You win a few; you lose a few." I feel this resembles the twin flame journey or any journey you are embarking on, as you cannot always make someone happy just because you are making a choice. At the end of the day, we need to learn to love ourselves enough to agree to disagree as that is what makes us unique individuals. All in all, we are here to follow our dreams and desires and to be able to trust our own intuition enough to set strong boundaries and be okay not to always agree with everything and learn to rein back our power to make better decisions for ourselves. The song that comes to mind that I feel relates to this chapter as well is "Put a Little Love in Your Heart." The song is a great reminder that before we can love someone else, we must love ourselves. The more we can do this, the more we will have a loving world. Instead of constantly looking outside ourselves for love, when we stop and listen to our hearts, we realize that we have always had love within ourselves. The more love we give ourselves, the more we are able to freely offer unconditional love to our children and all of humanity. This I know is a lesson we are constantly learning as we are incarnating here on Earth to pour the love into ourselves first before pouring it out to anyone else.

One picture that comes to mind is when I went to Washington, D.C., and I came across a poster that said, "Speak. Do not be silenced." I feel that these words are a reminder for all humans and for all people who are experiencing awakenings on a soul level that we need to be conscious of not silencing those around us as everyone's voice matters. I feel this message correlates with this chapter of incarnation as we humans are constantly learning on a conscious level to be mindful of letting people speak their minds instead of silencing them. Furthermore, another important aspect about the idea of incarnation is something we are reminded of at church on Sundays. The Apostles' Creed is a prayer in the Bible, which teaches us about incarnating. The Virgin Mary was chosen to incarnate with Joseph to create Jesus. We learn from this Biblical script to trust our own process of incarnation. I feel this shows that we are born into who we are, to be whole with ourselves, and to continue to forgive ourselves and one another. That is why we have lessons to learn along the way here on Earth to grow, evolve, and ascend into the person we are becoming.

The more we can learn these lessons, the more quickly we can ascend into the person we are becoming and do God's work for the greater good of humanity. Many religions and spiritual practices have a similar prayer to recognize that the reason we all incarnate here on planet Earth is to know that no one except God has the power over us and that we are powerful humans living out our soul lessons. I am being reminded of the coffee mug my dad had and his favorite saying: Nobody's Perfect. This is so true and the more we can adopt this in our reality, the better chance we have to allow for the fact that we live in an imperfect world. Things in life do not go perfectly and this is our opportunity to love and redeem ourselves.

CHAPTER 9

Connection in the Afterlife

This chapter is about the experience of meeting your twin flame and perhaps wanting to come together on a physical level right away or at points along the way. We must remember that we must completely surrender several times along this journey. Some twin flames do come together in the physical although some, who still have belief systems and patterns to work through, will further connect in the afterlife/heaven to continue to work together. As I mentioned in my previous incarnate chapter, we twins agreed before we came here that at some point when we are ready to meet, we would meet and spiritually work together or simultaneously work on our mission. When first meeting your twin flame, the twin flame is all butterflies and the icing on the cake is wanting to be with your twin flame both spiritually and physically.

Most twins do have a difficult time coming together physically as we must break the old ancestral patterns and work through our own grief. When meeting your twin flame, the journey highlights a lot of the grief you have not yet dealt with and must come face to face with to heal. That is why it is best to surrender and be still to the connection as the connection is about guiding one another toward the gifts that God has bestowed upon you. Some twin flames can come together although it depends on the amount of work you each work on individually. I am writing this as a guide as there are more twin flames that are meeting nowadays, and when you first meet, you experience a bubble love phase which quickly dwindles in six to eight weeks, only to find yourself having your world turned upside down as mine was. However, this upheaval can be for the better as, in my case, it sent me to do a lot of soul searching. Soul searching, like grief, takes lifetimes to process because you are only meant to do work a little at a time to heal wounds. A lot of twin flames also have a lot of ancestral wounds that need to be healed and you cannot heal overnight as it takes years to work through the wounded masculine and feminine energy we each have within us.

I decided to write this chapter as I met my twin flame when I was 46 and married and he was 59 at the time. As I mentioned above, you have a bubble love phase until the healing begins and the twin flames need to heal wounds of the past. At times, twin flames have to heal the way they look at love from the point of view of wisdom and knowledge, which makes this connection to one another polar opposites and helps us to balance the polarity in each of us. This is where the lessons of patience, balance, surrender, and respect for each other's viewpoint are important, while we continue to heal the suppressed parts of ourselves. We are meant to heal the patterns and false belief systems that we grew up with in our family lineage. We are continually healing the twin flame connection, learning how to lessen our expectations, and continuing to find the self-love within ourselves along this journey. This must unfold before we can support one another.

One of the things that we twin flames have learned to do is build up walls around love. We must continue to trust in ourselves, first and foremost, in order to best balance out the connection within each of us. I will not lie to you and tell you that the twin flame journey is all butterflies and roses. The journey can be about realizing that the more time you put into your own healing, the better you can create heaven on earth. At times, the twin flame journey can feel like an obsession as if you have made this connection up out of thin air only to get validation from within that you are not imagining it and that you must keep working on stepping into your spiritual gifts as you and your twin have your own life adventures to experience. You can either come together on all levels, if that is your soul plan, or continue working together in the afterlife/heaven. Our human ego side often wants to rush the connection although the soul always knows the way. The human ego will stop you from time to time from rushing the connection as you and your twin flame are always connected, no matter distance, space, or time.

The twin flame journey is a testament to faith, trust, and surrender to the twin flame connection. The twin flame journey is the ultimate sacrifice to be true to yourself and to be consciously aware of mindfulness on every level of mind, body, and soul. The common misconception right off the bat is when you meet your twin flame, you automatically crave the physical connection, only to find you are right on your healing path to discover the gifts and talents that each of you is gradually awakening to. As I mentioned, throughout this journey it is very important to surrender because, on a human level, we have grown accustomed to attaching to the outcome, but we must continue to trust and surrender our idea of how to achieve union with ourselves, Christ, and our twin flame. It will best come together by allowing the journey to unfold naturally. We, as humans, want to often take control rather than to let things naturally unfold. We must also put in the work to heal the wounds that have kept us suppressed over lifetimes.

My main reason for writing this chapter is to have you realize that you need to focus more on the 5d soul connection in this twin flame connection and to continue to focus on yourself as your twin flame is always a part of you. If we keep focusing on the 3d physical relationship connection, we must fully surrender and allow for the divine to work out how to have the 5d and 3d connection merge. Even though connected spiritually on a 5d level, we have to experience the 3d journey the way our soul is meant to and stand steady at times when we feel as though we are not in balance. The twin flame journey is always a conscious reminder of balancing all aspects of this journey on all levels despite where you and your twin flame are in the connection. One twin flame may be further along although the other twin eventually is not far behind, so that is why it is so important for surrender and self-care along this journey. We can continually balance out the connection with our twins and have union with ourselves, Christ, and our twin in whichever way the divine is orchestrating the divine union.

CHAPTER 10

Grief

I am writing this chapter on grief on the day after Lisa Marie Presley's passing and the same day that my twin flame Charley and I met for coffee. My reason for writing this chapter is that all twin flames who have met know that we go through several merges with our twin flame. One of the merges I have mentioned in the past is the connection through the eyes. The other merge that twin flames go through is a merge through the heart chakra. In this chapter, I am addressing the issue of experiencing oneness in union with my twin flame through the heart chakra which is a lifelong process that cannot be rushed. I am writing this through the lens of grief as well as the twin flame connection. Through the perspective of twin flames, when we go through a merging of the heart chakra, it can be an amazing experience. It can also cause both fear and anxiety, especially if it is something you have never experienced. Sometimes, as we go through the twin flame connection or any connection, we build walls up around love. At times, the twin flame journey can create a feeling of a deep sense of grief, much like when a loved one has passed. At times, the connection to your twin can be challenging when you have blocks to love. For many years, we have grief stuck in our bodies because we run away from love, instead of embracing love. As my teacher David Kessler says, "Grief is love and if you choose to love, your grief is part of love."

Sometimes we tend to avoid love, so we can avoid grief and feeling vulnerable. At times, through grief and the twin flame connection, we tend to run and hide to avoid how we love. During my twin flame connection, at times I have suppressed my emotions, only to feel them weeks or months down the road. Sometimes, twin flames have blocks to love, which feels like a deep grief much like a death. Instead of running away from love, we need to sit and be still with our emotions and work through blocks of love.

My yoga teacher Paul Denniston helps people process grief through a method called Grief Movement. Through movement, breath, and sound, Paul helps individuals who have grief stuck in their bodies to get their bodies moving and releasing unresolved grief that is held inside. Grief Movement helps to move suppressed emotions through. The twin flame connection relates to grief and blocking the connection through the heart. When twin flames have an unhealthy pattern in the way they observe love, it is hard to trust the connection.

The heart chakra merging is the process of coming home to oneness with yourself and your twin flame as well as the process of letting down the walls of love we build around love as we learn to embrace the connection to our twin flame. I want to highlight the fact that the more grief we let consume us, the more we have a hard time to balance out the other joys of life like fun, play, and laughter as laughter is the best medicine.

When going through the experience of merging your heart chakra with your twin flame, make sure you consciously use deep breathing through the merge rather than shallow breathing. If we tend to use a shallow breath, we end up feeling more anxiety or fear rather than peace and joy. The merging of the heart chakra should never be rushed as we also have to work on the layers of deep grief that we must release. Little by little it is important that you and your twin flame learn not to hold back because then you are suppressing your feelings and emotions which can lead to blocking your heart instead of opening your heart to one another or others in your lives. If you do not open your heart, you will always keep walls up around love and will not be able to trust in love. Because the twin flame connection can be strong, it can be an intense and yet a very peaceful journey, one with lots of unconditional love. The connection to your twin flame, when allowed, can unfold naturally and by being in the present moment, you can learn to balance your emotions and sit with your feelings rather than shutting down because of a fear of being vulnerable.

Life is too short, and we have only one life to live even though we live in different dimensions and realities. We have the now moment to embrace each merge through the heart chakra with love, peace, joy, and wisdom. When we learn to release layers of grief that we have not healed, we slowly merge heart chakras only when our souls are ready to do so. As I mentioned in one of the previous chapters on being an empath, empaths feel a lot of emotions. As for me, I will tend to shut down my emotions so as not to appear vulnerable, and then months later I will have to work through feelings of not having safely opened up. When you go through a heart merge with your twin flame, just remember to stay present with any emotions that may arise. You can even look around you and notice five observations about the environment to help you become present and aware of your surroundings, feelings, and emotions.

I felt moved to write this chapter, especially on this day in which there was a convergence of my meeting with my twin Charley and the untimely death of Lisa Marie Presley due to heart disease. Whatever we feel in the heart, we must feel it to heal it and not let anything go unsaid. We must trust ourselves and our heart connection as sometimes we get so stuck in our heads that we face a constant battle between the mind and heart. One thing that can be good is to connect with nature, as nature is oneness, and observe the surroundings of nature rather than be stuck in our heads, which causes us to spin out of control, often going round and round endlessly. Instead, we can benefit from just being in the pause and not attaching too much to expectations.

As an empath writing this, it is a lifelong practice to feel from the heart and embrace love rather than fear. Empaths will pick up emotions of others although it is important to remember that you can stay conscious of others and their emotions but not take them on as your own. David Kessler and Paul Denniston have taught me so much about staying present but detached. As David Kessler likes to say, "Be like a GPS or stay in your own lane." The more consciously you are aware of this, the more you can recognize and go within, figuring out if it is your own fears or the fears of someone else you are picking up and rein in your own energy.

This week I attended the funeral of my friend Bette. Through knowing my friend, I learned an important lesson about letting go of resentment and not holding on to these negative feelings. It was a lesson about the effect of blocking love and the resentment this causes although through the years Bette learned to just let it go. Yes, she was bothered by the resentment that was thrown her way in her life although she did not let that bother her as she found joy through the years and realized not to take on the resentment someone had towards her. This situation was a huge lesson as an empath not to hold on to resentment and to find joy in the small moments in life. Both resentment and grief can block the heart chakra. Working on past resentment is a necessity to set us free to enjoy our lives because if we hold on to resentment, it just keeps us in a prison.

I have learned to let go of resentment to find the joy, the love, and the heart connection we have with others. You must allow yourself to continue being in your own creative and authentic place and to love yourself within. Love and acceptance for yourself as you go through grief on any journey is to remember that with more love comes greater joy; it is better than holding on to resentment and blocking love. Empaths tend to want to give and then become resentful, so it is all about the balance of receiving and giving and working through emotions and feelings, rather than being consumed by them. We must strive not to skirt around or sweep feelings and emotions under the rug and to work through the feelings and emotions as they arise instead of dying with a broken heart. Sometimes, we convince ourselves that we may as well stay quiet and not express our feelings in a more creative and authentic way. This will not serve us fully.

I appreciated having the opportunity this week to learn these lessons from Charley my twin flame, Bette whose funeral I attended, and David Kessler my grief teacher who reinforces the idea that we must go through the grief and learn to achieve balance on any journey we embark upon. On the same day that I met my twin flame Charley for coffee, a song came on the radio at the bank called "God Only Knows," by King and Country. The song was profound and it reminded me that God is in control of any journey especially through grief or your twin flame connection. We do not have to judge ourselves or others. God is on our side and we can learn to love ourselves and God in the journey and remember that he has all the answers, so we do not need to try to be in control. We just need faith and trust in him. The song was a good reminder not to judge or even look outside ourselves when we are with God and we have the answers within.

We often just rely on one another and look outside ourselves for answers; we need to start believing, trusting, and loving ourselves from within as we go through our lives. God knows us better than anyone. We can express ourselves through his love and remember to have patience in grief as well as along the twin flame journey as it takes years to heal. David Kessler teaches that we need to feel things fully, we should drop the judgment around patience, and we can't skip the struggles by going around them. He also explains that the more of what you resist persists, so we can benefit from learning the lesson of resentment and having patience on the twin flame journey as we remember that one twin may be further along in the journey than the other. We learn through patience to look for the lessons of love instead of blocking love with resentment, always acknowledging that everyone does things at his or her own pace.

CHAPTER 11
Relationships

Where do I start? Well, let me begin with how I met my soulmate when I was working at Babson College. I had all these feelings for Bob Cirame, my manager at the time. I judged myself for having feelings for him and would do everything to suppress my emotions, even drinking and taking diet pills just to mask my feelings, hoping they would somehow disappear. Due to the culture of my family, I was taught from a young age to suppress my feelings and emotions. I was raised to believe that it was *not okay to feel your feelings.* When the manager for whom I had so many feelings got married, I felt so heartbroken and for many years had a hard time getting over him which is when I received the message to write a book.

Well, here I am now writing the relationships chapter of my twin flame book which has been long overdue. When I heard the call to write a book, I did not know what to write and, at first, did not heed the call to write. Years later, after not listening to the call right away to write, I met a person who mirrored back to me how unworthy I was. At first, I thought any relationship was better than nothing at all. I learned quickly as years went on in the early 2000s that I could not fix this man who struggled with a drug addiction. In my soul I knew that I deserved better. Yet, with my empathic nature, I thought I was the one who could fix him. I began to realize that I was unable to fix him or anyone, for that matter, yet having feelings of unworthiness and being an empath propelled me to continue to try. I would soon understand that this was a toxic relationship and that the only person I could help was myself.

Since the pandemic in 2020, I came upon David Kessler and Paul Denniston online. Over the years I have learned from David Kessler, my grief teacher, that you need to tend to your own garden and stay in your own lane, that no one needs fixing, and that we are not broken. Growing up, my dad shared a similar saying: mind your own business. I could never understand this until David Kessler reiterated a similar message over the last couple of years: stay in your own lane. I have slowly been integrating this. We are all so used to looking outside ourselves when the answer is within.

Next, after my relationship with the man who was addicted to drugs ended, I met my husband Abdul, whom I thought I could take care of. I soon realized that we were our own individual selves and that I could not control or fix him either. My desire to try to fix others and to be subservient to family seems to come out of my feelings of unworthiness as a young child. In doing my inner work, I have realized that I have carried over these feelings into my adult relationships, including my marriage to Abdul. It has all stemmed from being empathetic as well as not feeling safe to express how I feel.

About seven to eight years into my marriage, I met my twin flame Charley. Again, I recognized him on a soul level. Years after, we parted ways when my son finished preschool in 2016; I still had all these feelings for him and tried again to push down my feelings. I vowed I would never go back to drinking or taking diet pills to suppress my feelings rather than finding ways to express my emotions in a healthier way. Quickly, just as with my feelings for Bob Cirame, I could not get my mind off this man Charley. I wondered if this was another infatuation. Then I came across the term twin flames. At first, I vowed to myself that I would not attach to this label, but soon I began to better understand the meaning, ultimately choosing *Twin Flames* for the title of my book. Mary Magdalene and Jesus are twin flames as they incarnated as people who have met on the earth. Some people get so attached, as I did, to the label of twin flames, yet I knew there was something bigger than just attaching to a label which is something I have always been accustomed to doing in my life.

When I first met Charley, I thought right away this must be a physical romance, realizing years into doing a lot of inner work that some twin flames can come together on a physical level. The twin flame journey and connection to your twin flame is not just a physical union. Yet, when you have misconceptions of what love is, you automatically attach to the way in which you have been taught. The whole point first and foremost of the twin flame journey is to teach us how to come home to ourselves and discover the lost parts of ourselves, the strength and power within us, that we may have felt that we gave away or suppressed. Twin flames are here for unconditional love. What I mean is that we love ourselves and our twin flame counterparts along with loving all parts of ourselves and our twin flames — we accept the flaws in ourselves and in our twin flames and have no expectations of how the journey is meant to come together. You both are connected, yet on paths to finding the lost parts of yourself.

As my grief teacher David Kessler says, "Expectations are resentments under construction." The more I listen to this, the more I learn to integrate it. This is so true as I feel that growing up I, and many of us, have this notion that we have expectations of others that may not be realistic. We are all sovereign beings and we have the right to choose what is right for ourselves. As I continue to heal expectations and do my best to stay in my own lane as an empath, I know that the only person who can love me and fill my cup of love is myself. I cannot fix anyone and no one needs fixing. As Louise Hay mentions in her videos and podcast, it takes many lifetimes to heal and create new patterns of healing. She mentions that we, as humans, do hit plateaus on occasion and either decide to stay stuck or get unstuck by continuing the healing process. As David Kessler and Paul Denniston say that you can't go around only half healing, that healing takes lifetimes, and that to fully heal you must feel rather than run away.

So, why am I writing the relationships chapter after about thirty plus years of being asked by God to write a book and not knowing where to start? Perhaps the answer lies in experiencing this twin flame dynamic, being married at the time of meeting my twin flame, and understanding the other relationship dynamics that I have encountered. One thing that comes to mind is being mindful in all relationships to friendship, family, marriage, twin flames and being aware of the codependent patterns we tend to carry. Attachment and trying to enable someone are forms of codependency. From childhood, many people have learned to cope with personal issues by using mechanisms of codependency. It takes years to heal codependent patterns of behavior. It can be done as long as you are willing to heal and take an honest look at where codependency shows up in your life, for example by supporting someone's drug habit to acting like the other cannot think or do for him or herself.

Most recently, I decided wholeheartedly that I can love my twin flame Charley unconditionally, not placing demanding expectations on him, and learn to be with this connection as well as to heal what needs to be healed through the twin flame dynamic. I am also committed to healing anything that needs to be healed in my marriage to Abdul. One of the things that I am healing is my communication style as I have always had a hard time communicating my needs in a civilized manner. Rather, I am committed to understanding what my needs are and how I can balance and harmonize my needs as I have been so other oriented rather than focusing on self. Being in the twin flame dynamic, you learn to take a deeper dive into the abyss to find out who you are as a person.

Through the years, and as I am writing this chapter, I have been listening to Louise Hay and her wise words about how to start over. We are only human and it is up to us not to give up and to begin again. For highly sensitive empaths, like myself, cleansing our energy is important in order not to feel depleted. As Anita Moorijani mentions in her books, *Sensitive is the New Strong* and *Dying to Be Me*, being sensitive is our greatest strength, yet taking on too much energy will deplete us if we keep giving from an empty cup. In the relationship section, I want to express that, whatever dynamic you are in — self-care, love — compassion of self is most important and the importance of quieting ourselves and finding the time and place to recharge our battery or discover the parts of ourselves that we want to nurture. We often give away our power to others. Taking some time for introspection, we discover ways in which we keep playing small, hiding in fear, or running from ourselves because we have had the long-held belief that we are not worthy of love for ourselves or another.

Further, I want to highlight the fact we are worthy of receiving love and abundance on all levels. We also have to constantly work with the critic within us to tame thoughts of feeling unworthy as somewhere in our belief system we were taught to take care of others and put ourselves last. Being in a twin flame dynamic or in any relationship dynamic further highlights the need for self-love and to heal ourselves from within. As an empath, when growing up you long to find the lost parts of yourself without letting friends and family label you. Our empathic ways, if we do not know how to work with them and we keep giving of ourselves, can become a detriment. As Moorijani best describes in *Dying to Be Me*, we must learn to know how to filter out what our energy is and what someone else's energy is. Many twin flames are highly sensitive and learn to attract energy of all kinds, so knowing how to cleanse your own energy and take a lot of alone time to center yourself is vital. In any relationship, whether it be a twin flame dynamic, marriage, friendships, or family, taking care of our inner and outer selves is of the utmost importance as we cannot keep giving if our tank is empty.

In this chapter, I want to highlight the importance of belief systems. We tend to recreate the ones our parents have taught us. Belief systems are made to be challenged in order for us to create new ones. Rather than recreating the belief systems that our parents taught us, creating new belief systems actually helps in our growth and evolution process. Writing about beliefs in the relationship section is important because when we are in a relationship to self and others, some of the belief systems that once were true for us will no longer stick. We may be able to hold on to a few beliefs that we learned, yet we are meant to find and learn to create our own beliefs and what works and what does not. This is how we as members of a society can start to appreciate one another and learn from one another. Unconditional love exists when we can appreciate each other and our individual points of view rather than feeling we must hide for fear that someone will not agree with our beliefs. This is what makes each and every one of us unique.

As I am writing this chapter while sitting in Starbucks, the Whitney Houston song, "How Will I Know?" is playing. The song speaks about how you dream of someone, then you look into the person's eyes, which is a common theme when you have met your twin flame. And how when looking into their eyes you feel as if you are being transported to another dimension. The song also talks about how if this love is strong, why do I feel weak? This song represents any relationship, especially in a twin flame connection, as the energy between twin flames is strong and being vulnerable can make a person feel weak even if being vulnerable is very courageous. When meeting your twin flame, the dynamic can feel intense at times as lots of twin flames share the same soul frequency and you both mirror the same experiences that you have shared throughout life. What I mean by this is that your twin flame may have experienced something you are going through or went through, so that is why this twin flame dynamic can be intense as you both are meant to activate one another for mutual growth and evolution.

The song also talks about wondering if another person really loves us. On a soul level we love one another unconditionally, although on a human level the love that you feel for your twin can feel intense as it is meant to clear out the old ancestral belief patterns that are no longer meant to exist. When you are going through trust issues, grief from losing your twin in the past, as well as doubt about the relationship in the present, can arise from time to time. These feelings are all valid when you and your twin flame and people close to you — whether family or friends — will activate you to heal and grow. All in all, do not doubt your connection to your twin flame even though our human side is sometimes tired of the activations. The activations are meant to heal ancestral wounds we keep carrying that must be released. At times, there may be a pattern that we thought we cleared and healed, only to face the pattern again on a deeper level.

Most recently, I took a class with David Kessler and Dr. Frank Andersen, who teach about grief and trauma. Dr. Frank Andersen has a book called *Transcending Trauma: Healing Complex PTSD with Internal Family Systems.* Richard Schwartz is the founder of Internal Family Systems, which relate to the relationship we have to ourselves and to others. For so long, we, as individuals in society, have experienced trauma, and we may have developed codependent behaviors when our parents were not able to take responsibility for themselves, let alone their children. Then, as children, we have been taught to assume caretaking responsibilities. For instance, some children live with adults who struggle with life's demands. Sometimes these children are put into inappropriate caretaking positions, and as a result they develop codependent behaviors which may affect them their future adult relationships.

Through taking the class on Internal Family Systems and now understand that, due to my childhood interactions with family members, I had distorted boundaries which then led to confusing boundaries in my adult relationships. On a soul level, I knew the relationship was unhealthy, yet my human experience was affected by unclear boundaries and I believed it was better to mask and suppress my feelings and hide my true self. Through the study of Internal Family Systems, we learn to slowly accept our possibly skewed sense of self when we can identify and even appreciate the parts of self that felt violated as children. As an vital part of the relationship chapter, I feel it is important to share what I have learned through understanding Internal Family Systems as it provides an opportunity to know and understand how to work with the sense of self developed in childhood as a means to slowly heal aspects of ourselves in adulthood. We can identify the parts of us from which we keep running and heal the trauma within. As Dr. Frank Andersen mentions in class, we must make an effort to make a U-turn in healing the parts of ourselves rather than attending to someone else's unhealed parts or running from our own to avoid the trauma that can be witnessed and healed.

Most recently, I heard a lecture by Richard Schwartz, author of the self-help book, *No Bad Parts*. Basically, the author's message is simple: When you go through a self-inventory to better understand and heal parts of yourself, you thank all parts of yourself as a way of acknowledging that we have no bad parts. It is through accepting and healing parts of ourselves that we can arrive at inner peace.

It is often the case that those of us on the twin flame journey, or any journey we are embarking upon, seek immediate gratification. The twin flame journey is more about growth and evolution than immediate gratification. We, as humans, are so used to immediate gratification as the ego wants everything in the now moment rather than to be patient. This was a huge epiphany for me not to get too upset and feel disappointed when my twin flame and I are not in complete physical union. You are both in union with one another on a spiritual level. The human side of us has lessons to master at a human level in order to integrate the spiritual and physical together which can take many incarnations. The more lessons that you and your twin flame, or any other type of relationship you are in, have, the more you are learning to bring together knowledge and wisdom to share with one another and with the world. This is when growth and appreciation for your twin flame, for yourself, and for the outer world can happen — when we can accept what each of us has to offer.

I know from experience that when I put pressure on myself, the ego is putting the pressure on my human side which then causes an imbalance of jealousy, anger, resentment, and hurried energy rather than staying heart centered. The soul always knows the way if we just allow ourselves to stay present.

In David Kessler and Dr. Frank Andersen's class on trauma and grief they touched on a bit of trauma bonding. We tend to trauma bond when we carry unhealed trauma. On the twin flame journey as we heal our wounds, sometimes we attract people who have unhealed parts of themselves, which is called trauma bonding. In any relationship we must be cognizant of trauma bonding and notice when we start letting people take from our energy. This is why it is so important as mentioned previously to cleanse our energy. Empaths especially have to be aware as they are the people who want to fix everything. Be mindful of when you are not tending to yourself. I share this chapter as a reminder to be mindful in your relationship to yourself and to others as you heal trauma and clear energies that no longer resonate with your belief system.

CHAPTER 12

Twin Flames and How They Change Your World

In Chapter 1, I describe how you don't go looking for your twin flame. They appear when you least expect it. Are we ever prepared for something that changes our world? Many times, throughout writing this book, I kept thinking of changing the title yet decided to keep the title as it was originally written for the very fact that twin flames *really do* change and challenge the world you once knew. Twin flames are meant to help one another, and eventually the collective, to grow and evolve. At times when people have sporadic communication with their twin flames, they will sometimes question the truth of the twin flame journey. It is my hope that this book will encourage you to stay on course with faith throughout the twin flame journey.

Recently, there has been a release of a documentary presenting many falsehoods about the twin flame experience, making a mockery of the twin flame phenomenon. In the documentary, the leader claims that he has all the answers to someone's twin flame journey, a bold assertation which is very ego driven. The answer to your twin flame journey lies within you and God or a power you pray to greater than yourself. As my writing teacher Andrea Cagan one time mentioned, run in the other direction when someone says they know you better than you know yourself. Her mentioning this is a reminder to trust your intuition. We must remember the twin flame journey or any spiritual journey helps you pause and completely do a U-turn into the abyss to eradicate the pieces that you have kept hidden inside yourself and illuminate the light within you. Twin flames come together for sporadic communication as it is meant to help you with inner expansion like an accordion. The sporadic communication can feel sometimes as if you are imagining the twin flame connection in your mind, only to then go into the heart, and that's why it feels raw and uncontrollable. You may feel as though you are not changing, yet each step of the way you are. That is why it is good to pause and breathe and remember you can only change a little at a time and change does not happen overnight.

The twin flame journey is a spiritual love that transcends all dimensions and realities. Meeting and interacting with your twin flame will change your world. It reminds us that the experience not only brings unconditional love, but it also brings you back to your soul's blueprint. You and your twin flame are on a path of awakening to discover yourselves while never being separated from one another as you, along with your twin flame, God, and the rest of the world, are not separate even though the journey can bring up the dark night of the soul or a deep feeling of loneliness bringing you to your knees for the millionth time. You and your twin even though you are on a path of self-discovery are with each other internally slowly merging in God's time and not your time.

You and your twin are a part of one another similar to a twin brother or sister where you are whole on your own but never separated from your twin and God or God source. Even though you may not yet be physically together you are always working in tandem with one another on a spiritual level. This is why I decided to keep the book title: Twin Flames and How They Change Your World. This journey does literally *challenge your world* in breaking down the old belief systems that you were so accustomed to, only to find the new version of you.

The day of January 6th when I sent the last chapter to my editor, I met a girl wearing a twin flame sweatshirt in Panera in Needham, Massachusetts. The significance of this experience is twofold. As mentioned in an earlier chapter, my son's preschool teacher was my twin flame and before I would take my son to preschool, I would sometimes go to the same Panera in Needham. Then, seeing the design of two flaming hearts together on the back of the girl's sweatshirt was such synchronicity and sums up what twin flames are all about—we are connected through the heart with lots of fiery passion and we are one with one another!

Each twin flame pair stirs the heart and sets your passions on fire in order to dismantle the old and bring in the new, to help humanity to awaken one moment, one day, and one step at a time.

CHAPTER 13

A coming home to oneself

I wanted to include this chapter to write fully why the Twin flame Journey is a coming home to oneself. In the chapter on Empathy I speak about helping my mom through grief. What I meant was when you are on a spiritual path such as Twin flame or any other spiritual path you come across a modality called womb healing. Womb healing helps you to release any energy that you may have absorbed in the womb. Mine was the grief my mom experienced when she lost her sister and brother in law in an automobile accident while she was pregnant with me. So womb healing is one way in which can help free you from carrying the grief that you may have from the womb. In chapter 12 I spoke briefly and wanted to expand on was the documentary that came out a year ago on Netflix about the twin flame cult that made a mockery and twisted what the twin flame path is all about which is a coming home to oneself. I know as I almost joined after my mom had passed away in 2018 and I had very little contact with my twin flame and has just been 2 years on the twin flame path so I was searching for any answer to fill my logic mind. Thankfully I had amazing angels watching over me as well as my intuition guiding me not to fully invest in the twin flames universe cult. I joined for a brief time yet it just felt it was not in alignment with who I was as they just wanted to control the people in the group promising them they would help them find their twin flame. As I mentioned you don't go looking with your twin flame. They appear when you both are ready to heal the dynamics of ancestral healing and the share the unconditional love that resides within each of you. Once I saw this group for who they were I cancelled my membership and as I did the cult leader basically told me if I cancelled my membership that I would never find love which was one of his many false accusations and one that does not align in the twin flame connection. I guess I needed to experience that in order for the codependency to heal from the ancestral pattern that my twin and I agreed to heal through our connection. Through the twin flame journey the coming home to oneself happens throughout and you learn a little about yourself as you unravel layers of yourself that you always kept hidden. Most recently I joined a church choir as I love to sing. The choir director Charlie Kanelos really helped to open up my voice up to music and in general to speak up. This was one way I was able to find my voice instead of hide away. I did not realize how much the choir I loved because before I joined I felt I was always doing things to fit in rather than to find who I was. The twin flame journey will help you discover the lost parts of ourselves as we are all unique and we can learn from one another's experience instead of fitting in. I want to also recognize my kindred spirit and best friend Michael Auclair for always helping me to find my voice and speak up for justice. This too help me unravel layers I never thought I had in which I knew I have had yet it is one day at a time process.

Printed in the United States
by Baker & Taylor Publisher Services